A SHORT HISTORY
OF MUSIC

THIRD AMERICAN EDITION
REVISED

A SHORT HISTORY OF

MUSIC

by ALFRED EINSTEIN

TRANSLATED FROM THE GERMAN

DORSET PRESS
NEW YORK

Published January 2, 1937

Second American Edition, revised and enlarged,
with 39 musical examples added,
October 31, 1938

Third American edition, revised, April 1947

Originally published as *Geschichte der Musik*
Copyright 1934 by
A. W. Sijthoff's Uitgeversmij N. V. — Leiden

This edition published by
Dorset Press,
a division of
Marboro Books Corporation,
by arrangement with
Alfred A. Knopf, Inc.

1986 Dorset Press.

ISBN 0-88029-097-8

Printed in the United States of America

M 9 8 7 6 5 4

PREFACE

THIS CONCISE HISTORY OF MUSIC, which has passed
through three editions in Germany and one in Hol-
land, was first produced some thirty years ago. It was
written in a few weeks, at a time and place that pre-
cluded resort to any books of reference. Lists of names
and dates, however, were not my object; my desire
was to present a picture of the development of music
as a whole, the historical form of that development,
and the figures of a few of the great masters. The
reader will, I venture to hope, appreciate a certain unity
in this presentation, which a mass of details would have
destroyed.

The work was originally one of a popular educational series, and as such its scope was very limited. But
it never really fitted its frame, for it is not exactly an
educational book. It is addressed rather to the reader
who has already made himself acquainted with some of
the facts of musical history and has heard pre-classical,
classical, romantic, and modern music performed —
heard it attentively. Of what value to a reader is a history of music unless music is part of his experience?
And music of the present as well as of the past. The

music of the present explains that of the past, and not the other way round. Of what use to a blind man is a history of art?

None of the later editions of the present book, either in German or in English, is like the first one. I tried to emend and to correct it in every case. This is true especially for the musical examples, of which several have been replaced by more characteristic or typical ones in each edition.

It is perhaps not unnecessary to emphasize that the examples do not claim to demonstrate the development of music from the beginnings until now. Their aim is simply to furnish representative models of old music to which the reader of today has not as easy access as he has to the music of the classics and romantics. They are necessarily short. Shortness was also imperative in the notes: every piece of old music may be analyzed from several points of view.

ALFRED EINSTEIN

Note on the TRANSLATION

THE TRANSLATION is the work of several hands. Of the collaborators undernamed some have contributed a few and others many pages. All have undertaken the task as a pleasure for the opportunity it afforded of paying their respects to the esteemed author.

ERIC BLOM

MARIANNE BROOKE

RICHARD CAPELL

H. C. AND HESTER COLLES

EDWARD J. DENT

EDWIN EVANS

A. H. FOX STRANGWAYS

WILLIAM GLOCK

SCOTT GODDARD

P. HOPE-WALLACE

DYNELEY HUSSEY

ROBERT L. JACOBS

MARION M. SCOTT

J. A. WESTRUP

BERYL DE ZOETE

London, 1936

CONTENTS

CONTENTS

x

Contents

xi

A SHORT HISTORY
OF MUSIC

PRIMITIVE MUSIC

THE FIRST beginnings of music lie even deeper in historical obscurity than those of speech, the relics of which are very much older. The only means of throwing any light on the subject is afforded by the observation of musical development in children and the music of primitive peoples. To the man who in prehistoric times first perceived musical sound as it originated in the beating of a hollow object or by the swing and whir of a staff, it was something in-

3

comprehensible and therefore mysterious and magical. The mere sound of percussion instruments excited him to the pitch of intoxication. From them he discovered the power of rhythm, which inflamed and ordered the ritual dance and also co-ordinated the movements of labour and, as if by magic, lightened toil. At the same time man may have acquired practice in the use of notes of definite pitch for signals in war, since they differ markedly from the ill-defined tones of speech in virtue of their distinctness. From that he may soon have hit upon a preference for the most sonorous and " easy " intervals, the fourth and fifth. To tone and rhythm was added primitive melody, in conjunction with more or less intelligible words, in the first place probably as a magic initiation-formula of priests in religious rites or in the song of a chorus-leader in dancing or at work. At the same time individuals may have been stimulated to satisfy through musical sounds their emotional needs, pleasurable or the reverse. A characteristic of the conception of primitive music is monotony, the endless repetition of the same short melody, just as the alternation of solo and chorus, improvisation and a regular refrain are among the oldest ingredients of musical form.

Natural science has tried to discover a prehuman origin for music in the song of birds; and comparative musicology, which deals with the prehistoric development of music, has admitted that primitive

4

man may have been attracted by bird-song in the first place and have continued to use it as a model for imitation. What is certain is that the practice of music among primitive peoples shows a continual movement between two opposite extremes, excitement and repose; its typical form is therefore melody that begins on a high note and then sinks or falls to a definite final or tonic. Attempts have been made to determine the period at which such melodies originated on the basis of the range of their musical material — a limited range suggesting an early date, and so on — but without any certainty. Solo and choral song may have existed side by side from the very beginning. Whereas, however, solo song is prepared to take almost any liberties and follows the dictates of freedom — freedom, not mere caprice or absence of rhythm — combined choral singing, whether at work or dancing, presupposes rhythmic unity; and this contrast is found even in primitive music. The combined singing of men and women and the simultaneous sound of voice and some such instruments as the pan-pipes may often have produced at quite an early date a kind of rude, unintentional polyphony — or rather heterophony; that is, arbitrary ornamentation of the same melody by several performers at the same time — and a combination of several rhythms.

THE ANCIENT
CIVILIZATIONS

It is characteristic of primitive melody that the intervals were few, small, and, especially, indefinable and variable. The music of early civilizations is differentiated from the music of nature by the recognition of the octave and all that it involves; by the impulse to tackle theoretically the problem of finding points of emphasis in the tones and semitones into which they divided the scale and, in particular, in its two complements, the fourth and the fifth; and by the consolidation of melody. The pentatonic scale stands as a token of an early stage of this endeavour. This scale is limited to five degrees of the octave, and the less easily compassed semitones are avoided, much as a child avoids and replaces by easier ones the difficult sounds of a language. To this fanciful or expressive use of tones and scales was added actual mathematical measurement, which led to the discovery — beyond the natural divisions of the octave — of mechanical and artificial divisions. These strange, queer systems stand to the natural scales less as rudiments than as degenerations consecrated by convention; and on them were built most refined types of melody which leave us with the impression of an art at once immature and over-ripe.

The pentatonic or, more accurately, the non-semitonal scale may be accepted as the rudimentary basis of every other tonal system throughout Europe and Asia, and it is recognizable in all the records we possess of primitive music. Of music in ancient Egypt we know too little, in spite of an abundance of pictorial illustrations, to be able to say definitely whether it was adopted in this ancient cradle of culture at the meeting-place of three continents. But in China the development from the non-semitonal to the seven-note scale is certainly traceable, even though the old pentatonic always remained the foundation of its music. In Japan beside the original scale we have a series of peculiar pentatonic scales, in which semitones are employed. In Java the octave is divided into five, or seven, equal degrees, which have no relation to the intervals that we regard as natural.

The musical culture of the Near East is quite different from what may be called in a particular sense "Oriental," that of India and Arabia and Persia. In India the normal seven-note octave is the basis of all melody; but it becomes transformed and overgrown by a whole host of minute intervals employed for the sake of ornament. The Arabic-Persian system is even further removed from ours; it is built up of small units of a third of a tone — originally seventeen and later twenty-four to the octave — and shows the influence of Greek musical theory. Both these peoples have in common a natural disposition for making music, which is partly mystical and partly emotional. Both distinguish between solemn, religious music, which admits the greatest variety in the structure of rhythm and melodies and is frequently independent of speech-rhythm, and music of the folk, in which melodic restraint is often carried to the point of rigidity, and the symmetrical grouping of the smallest melodic units or motives is popular. Both, also, have astonishingly elaborate instrumental resources, from percussion instruments handled with great virtuosity to every kind of wind

8

and string instrument, plucked and bowed. To Arabian music Europe owes the lute and the violin.

The ancient civilization which has given us supreme examples of the plastic arts acted in music as a mediator in the most spiritual sense between the traditions of East and West. For the Greeks, too, music was, as its name implies, a divine discovery. The followers of Orpheus and of Pythagoras still saw in music a magical means of purification and of healing. But from the Greek musical practice of early times to an ideal conception of the art the way was astonishingly short. They came to regard it as a necessary element of education and general culture. They even held it to be one of the pillars of political morality, believing that the State could no more than the individual dispense with right harmony and true rhythm. They placed music among the subjects in which open artistic competition was held during the ritual year at festivals, tribal or municipal; and besides these great occasions there were competitive games; above all, the Pythian games at Delphi, which were specially devoted to music: to the lyric contests, which consisted of the poetical and musical inventions called "nomoi"—the praises of the gods in the definite form of antiphonal melodic strophes, sonatas, as we might say, of pure melody; and, very early, to pure instrumental music. In 586 B.C., actually, the wind-player SAKADAS took the prize with a program symphony on the "aulos"

9

(a reed instrument, not a flute) which purported to represent the fight of the Pythian god with the dragon. But the highest form of this artistic competition was the drama, whose origin is to be sought in the dithyramb, the choral dance in honour of Dionysus. In tragedy and comedy — the union of music, poetry, and dance — the music took the form of solos for the actors and songs and dances for the chorus.

The Greeks recognized two sides to music — revelry, in the sense of elemental excitement, and spiritual uplift. They embodied these in the association and rivalry of music for the aulos, either independently or to give colour to choral song, and vocal music accompanied by the kithara. In the palmy days of tragedy accompanied by the aulos this rivalry was determined in favour of the instrument of revelry; and in this lay the inner meaning of Plato's ban on tragedy. The predominance of instrumental music, the neglect of speech, by which alone man could overmaster the dæmonic element imported by such music, the intrusion of the Eastern conception of music as a merely sensual incitement, the dictatorship of popular taste and mere virtuosity — it was to all this that the philosophic writers ascribed the downfall of the ancient art. We cannot test this judgment of theirs; but it happens that the movement of that downfall coincided with the complete enunciation of the æsthetic of antiquity, with the systems of harmony, rhythm, and acoustics which were to exert the greatest influence on posterity.

The " chromatic " and " enharmonic " of Greek music have nothing to do with the meanings we attach to those words nowadays, nor does their " harmony " imply music in several parts or anything like modern polyphony. The mere facts that tone and word were inseparable and that the musician's time-unit depended on the poet's prosody preclude any thought of ancient polyphony. Greek music was purely monodic. The accompaniment by their favourite kithara, and by the aulos too, did not amount to more than ornamentation of the vocal melody and connecting notes, and occasionally to the playing of certain intervals. Greek " harmony " is a doctrine of melody — of melody so fully and finally developed as to be a convincing refutation of any harmony in our sense. The basis of Greek melody is a scale-theory consisting of tetrachords differentiated by the position of the semitone. These, written in accordance with Greek feeling and theory in descending form, are: Dorian, A, G, F, E; Phrygian, A, G, F♯, E; and Lydian, A, G♯, F♯, E. A further distinction of these elements was made by the three genera: diatonic, A, G, F, E; chromatic, A, F♯, F, E; and enharmonic, A, F, F<, E. Melody so minutely developed as this, bound by fixed laws but susceptible of abundant modulation — that is, combining the various modal species — implies in its hearers an exceptional sensibility for melodic and rhythmic detail; and this in its turn derives from a long and intricate symbolism of interval, with its roots deep in history — from the character (*ethos*) of the different octave-scales. This sensibility is suggested also by the fact that they were content with the few strings of the kithara, giving a compass of about eleven notes, and their weak-toned reed instrument — a very different state of things from ours. The Greeks had no bowed string instrument and despised the many-stringed harp of the Egyptians.

The most important of the Greek theoretical writers on music was the Peripatetic philosopher ARISTOXENUS OF TARENTUM (*c.* 320 B.C.), one of the advocates of the psychological study of music and an opponent of the speculative researches of the Pythagoreans, who were concerned with the science of acoustics. A compendium of classical theory was supplied by the Alexandrian writer CLAUDIUS PTOLEMÆUS (second century of our era); but the writers who actually passed on to the Middle Ages the Greek conception and doctrine of music were the late Roman " philosophers " Boethius and Cassiodorus, both of whom belong to the sixth century. In music, as in the other arts, the Romans were entirely unproductive and depended on the Greeks, whom they had made their subjects.

There have come down to us a few short melodies

of Greek music and fragments of longer ones, though none of the virtuoso pieces in several sections; and these we can interpret, thanks to the notation being in two forms, vocal and instrumental. All these remnants show how difficult, how impossible it is for us to recover the expressive value of Greek music. The Middle Ages and subsequent times knew none of these discoveries or, if they did, could not decipher them. That was their good fortune. For the knowledge of the place music took as an ideal in Greek life, the marvel of this highly developed system, and the conclusion from these premises that their actual music was of a unique and exalted character — all this evaluation upon credit has, from the Middle Ages right down to Richard Wagner, had the most fruitful consequences, by blazing up at important crises and stirring men's minds, and all the more since there were no concrete examples of the music itself.

THE MIDDLE AGES

The Gregorian Chant

THE MIDDLE AGES are reckoned in general history to begin with the permanent establishment of a Germanic dominion at the centre of the Roman Empire. In the history of music the most characteristic feature of classical antiquity — monody — survived much longer. It can all the same be fully admitted that a new period of music began with the birth of Christendom. The Faith, or rather the Church, before whose expansive and conquering spiritual might Constantine bowed, while astutely

14

making use of it for his own purposes, had from its inception allowed music an important place in its liturgical exercises; and just as it adopted for its use contemporary forms of the representative arts, so it made no difficulty in taking over the musical tradition inherited from the pre-Christian world. The source of Christian liturgical song is to be sought, not at Rome, but in the Eastern provinces of the Empire. Until the end of the third century, Greek was the liturgical language of the new faith, and a relic of it survives in the Kyrie of the Roman Mass. The Christian ecclesiastical chant was first formulated at Jerusalem and in the Syrian and Alexandrine communities — particularly in monastic brotherhoods — and from the beginning Jewish and Greek influences were inextricably mingled. The incentives from the East, transmitted and kept alive by Byzantium, remained more or less active even in later times. It was particularly strong in the eighth century under popes of Syrian or Greek descent and continued to bear fruit under the Carolingians in France and Alemannia until brought to a close about 1050 by the Great Schism. Curiously enough, the Great Schism also marks the beginning of the lethargy and decadence of the vocal music of the Eastern Church, whereas the Western chant begins only then to bear its choicest blooms and progresses towards the hitherto unimagined glories of polyphony.

15

The offices of the Hours are the most ancient portion of the Christian liturgy, the singing of the psalms having been adopted from the Jewish synagogue. The actual performance also corresponded to the Jewish practice of psalmody. It was at first responsorial, consisting, that is to say, of solo-singing by the precentor, answered by the choir (Cantus responsorius). After the middle of the fourth century antiphonal singing, which had originated in the Syrian monasteries, came into general use. As the name indicates, it consisted of the singing of two choirs in alternation. These were at first contrasted in pitch — one being composed of men, the other of women or boys — and later similar. Women seem to have ceased to take part from a comparatively early date (c. 578).

Like the antiphons and responds which were associated with psalm-singing, there are hymns of Hellenistic origin which also belong to the earliest corpus of Church music. And like the antiphons, the hymns, too, are said to have been transplanted from the East into the Western Church by St. Ambrose, Bishop of Milan (d. 397), as representatives of a more popular mode of song, as the vehicles of a simpler melody. St. Ambrose took an active part as poet in the making of these hymns. Like the hymns of the Syrian St. Ephrem, they are important because of the change that took place in them from classical quantitative prosody to modern scansion by accent.

Rhyme, which appeared later, completed this transition. Psalmody, antiphons, responds, and hymns
were the elements that combined to form the complete musical setting of the liturgy, the form of
which was established by Gregory the Great (d.
604). Doubtless not without some basis in fact, tradition has it that the fourteen years of his papacy
were crowded with developments which only later
evolution may have brought to maturity: the collection and standardizing of the historical musical
formulas; the foundation or restoration in Rome of
a song-school entrusted with the task of preserving
and cultivating, in the purity of its tradition, the
wealth of liturgical song. From this establishment
was to ensue the dissemination throughout the entire Christian world of the authentic antiphonal. It
was very soon carried to Ireland and later into the
vast Frankish Empire. It was often modified or sim-
plified, but always restored. In fact, in course of
time other " dialects," so to speak, of ecclesiastical
song — the Gallican, for instance, in the Western
Frankish kingdom, and the Spanish (that is, Moz-
arabic) — had to give way before the Roman; and
only the Ambrosian preserved its minute and no
longer clearly definable particularities.

Western church music, or Gregorian song, was
bound up with a uniform cult-language, Latin. The
church song of the Eastern Roman Empire was
without this bond. It consisted of religious poetry

and music, which had grown up on national soil and consequently remained split up into a number of musical "dialects," such as the Syrian, the Byzantine, and the Armenian; and though these dialects were related, they were individually distinguished by the regions to which they belonged. Later came Russian church song, trailing in the rear of these developments; indeed, it might be described as a bastard child of Eastern church music, since not only "Greek" (or Byzantine) but also Slavonic blood flowed in its veins. In Byzantine church music the development of the "tropes" — short verses interpolated between the verses of the psalms — led to the creation of hymns, strophic poems, often of great length, which later, possibly in the seventh century, developed into the stricter and more elaborate "canons," as they were called. It was not till the tenth century that definite limits were set to the use of this rich store of poetry and melody in the liturgy, with the result that the poetical, though not the musical, development of the Byzantine hymn came to an end.

The contrasting styles of responsorial and antiphonal singing shaped the liturgical music of the whole of the Middle Ages, which derived its artistic life from them. Choral singing was by its very nature the vehicle of a simple, syllabic music and the representative of tradition, whereas solo-singing, with its delight in melismatic ornamentation, naturally challenged tradition and became the organ of progress. Singers who appeared to forget the impregnability of liturgical song might attempt to transform it, but in spite of them responsorial song continued to gain ground. It had its stronghold in the Mass, which, though all its details were not finally determined until the eleventh century, slowly rose to be the most richly equipped central element of the liturgy and took precedence over the offices of the Hours. And in the Church, congregational singing has tended to become restricted in favour of performance by a class of specially trained singers.

Solo-singing has indeed always had to deal with certain conflicting claims — between verbal stress and metrical accent and between pure melodic expression and declamation. Already St. Augustine was suspicious of the effect of richly melodic ornamentation. A particularly debatable field was the wordless Jubilus, the Alleluia-singing which Pope Damasus (d. 384) had introduced to the West from Jerusalem and which supplied the foundation of those curious interpolated songs, suggested by a Byzantine model, which from the ninth century were cultivated under the name of " proses " or " sequences " in the monasteries of western Europe. The melismatic extension of the Alleluia was replaced by texts syllabically adapted to definite poetic forms suitable for antiphonal singing. Perhaps the piety of the monks had been offended by the luxuriance of the melismatic element, or the object may have been to give a definite rhythmical construction to melodies otherwise difficult to remember; or possibly pious fervour demanded that the nature of a particular office or liturgy should be emphasized. The same spirit also gave rise to the tropes — syllabic interpolations ornamenting the music of the Mass. The principal author of sequences was NOTKER BALBULUS (d. 912), a monk of St. Gall, to whom the text of the antiphon *Media in vita in morte sumus* was for long erroneously attributed. Among his followers were Waltramus, Wipo, Berno von Reichenau, and Hermann the Lame. TUOTILO, author of tropes, was his contemporary and also lived at St. Gall. We shall see that in these syllabic interpolations, which took the place of the Oriental melismata, lay the seed of polyphony — the seed, too, of the liturgical drama, since many of these tropes, those for Christmas and Easter, for example, were treated as dramatic dialogues with question and answer. The popular tendency which the sequences revealed during their first rise in Alemannia soon gained strength, and the later sequence poems, such as those of ADAM DE ST. VICTOR (eleventh century), the *Dies iræ* of THOMAS DE CELANO, incorporated in the Requiem Mass, the magnificent *Stabat Mater*, probably by JACOPONE DA TODI (both of these dating from the thirteenth century), are, in both their literary and their musical form, popular hymns.

In spite of all subjective movements, Gregorian song has on the whole exhibited a remarkable constancy; and the Church was right in exercising over music in this instance an artistic control which it never again, and in no other field, insisted upon with the same obstinacy. The vitality, ever effective and ever renewed, of Gregorian melody is based upon its simplicity and purity; upon its melodic severity, by which it may also have differentiated itself from the melodic expression of pagan Rome, since the regularization of its melodic progress rests upon a simplification of the classical theory of melody; upon the distinguishing of four " authentic modes," the first D, E, F, G, A, the second E, F, G, A, B, the third F, G, A, B, C, the fourth G, A, B, C, D, with which the four " plagal modes " are connected by completion of the lower octave. Of these eight modes the authentic are to be regarded as a combination of the intervals of the fifth and fourth (D, A, D, etc.), the plagal as a combination of the fourth and fifth (A, D, A, etc.). The former create a feeling of rest and stability; in the latter there is a striving to come to rest. In mediæval theory they were given, inaccurately, the names of the classical scales. Together with these designations they acquired the definite ethical attributes which each of those scales was supposed to possess. These associations held good until the disappearance of the church modes and furnished important indications of the significance they expressed. Within these modes melodic formulas of Gregorian song were developed, and the distinct character of each mode is as evident from the preliminary intonation and final cadence as from the note chosen for the recitation. The typical Gregorian melody begins with the intonation, consisting of a definite formula, which rises to the monotone or reciting note; it remains on that note for a time and then descends again with a formal cadence. Though Gregorian song is necessarily restricted, there are numerous gradations of structure between the simple syllabic setting and the florid melismatic type, and to these it owes its abundance of forms, from the simplest song-melody to an elaborate organization that suggests comparison with the later sonata.

The early Middle Ages made a comprehensive study of the theoretical treatment of plainsong. The most complete formulation of principles was achieved in the eleventh century at the Reichenau Monastery in the writings of HERMANN THE LAME. Classical conceptions naturally played a large part in the establishment of theory. The most important of those who helped in the transmission of the legacy was, as I have already mentioned, the late Roman philosopher BOETHIUS (d. 526); from him was derived the conception of music that dominated the whole of the Middle Ages. Creative power was ranked below theoretical knowledge; and though this attitude helped to give music its place in the scholastic culture of the time, it was bound to introduce into living creation a strain of purely abstract artificiality.

The notation used for the Gregorian plainsong — that of the neumes — was vastly superior to the Greek system. Its function was to call to mind a comparatively small number of familiar types of melody. For that reason the exact definition of Greek notation was abandoned. The music being purely vocal, the notation dispensed with indications of rhythm; but it possessed an immediate intelligibility that was lacking in the Greek system, since it actually gave a visual representation of the rise and fall of the melody. It became the sure foundation on which modern notation was to be built; the one thing it lacked — the exact indication of intervals — was supplied by GUIDO D'AREZZO in the eleventh century. Anxious as he was to arrest the decay that was threatening the survival of church song, Guido hit on the simple but inspired device of fixing the pitch of the notes by means of lines a third apart. The non-representational system of letters and figures remained in force right down to the eighteenth century, but only for instrumental music — a quaint paradox, since the lines of the staff are actually nothing but the direct representation on paper of the strings of an instrument. Guido's "sol-mization" also provided the theoretical basis for a more fully developed system of composition. Thus at a time when music was still confined to monody the ground was already prepared for harmonic relations and the principle of transposition and modulation (or "mutation"); and this system remained in force for the next five hundred years.

Solmization is an extension of the classical theory of scales, in so far as it shows the relationships of notes — that is, the distinct position of the semitone in the scale — not in the tetrachord (series of four notes), but in the hexachord (series of six notes). The doctrine of solmization makes use of definite names for the notes — do, re, mi, fa, sol, la (whence the name "solmization"), and so at the same time indicates their individual functions. The three six-note scales, starting from what we call C, G, and F (the last with the fourth note of the scale flattened), all exhibit exactly the same relationships of tones and semitones and so all begin with "do." Modulation (or "mutation") always means that a note has changed its function in the scale, and with the change of function it naturally changes its name as well. Our modern methods of indicating notes by words, such as tonic sol-fa, are simply adaptations of solmization to our system of octaves, with its more extensive opportunities for modulation. Guido's complete scale consisted of twenty notes, from G on the first line of the modern bass staff to E on the fourth space of the treble. As an aid to learning it, students were given a memory-line which was in a literal sense " handy." It began at the extremity of the thumb and ran more or less in the form of a spiral over all the joints and tips of the fingers; it was known as the " Guidonian Hand." It was not till the beginning of the eighteenth century that this system received its actual death-blow (from Mattheson); but in practice it had disappeared much earlier, when the church modes gradually gave place to the establishment of the major and minor modes, as the normal constituents of tonality, about the year 1600.

Polyphony

When Gregorian plainsong was at its height, the most important event in the whole of Western musical history occurred: the birth of polyphony. This was nothing less than the beginning of that development of an art based on laws of part-writing and harmony to which we remain subject at the present day. The ancient world had, of course, often stumbled on the fact of harmonic consonance. The achievement of the Middle Ages was that men did not rest content with that fact, but used it to cultivate a seed that was to grow to a new and immeasurable harvest.

Rousseau called polyphony "a Gothic and barbarous invention." He was right in a deeper sense than he realized. The pleasure in harmonic consonance is indigenous to the folk-music of the Northern races. We do not know whether the "lurs" — similarly voiced bronze horns for calling to the assembly, constantly found in pairs and dating from long before the time of Julius Cæsar — emitted a two-part signal blast to the Germanic peoples on the western shores of the Baltic. It is certain that the Irish philosopher JOHANNES SCOTUS ERIGENA, about the middle of the ninth century, understood two-part singing (probably the Anglo-Saxon Aldhelm at the end of the seventh century already refers to it). If we may trust modern research, it seems not impossible that other European countries also knew polyphony in the early Middle Ages. All our actual evidence, however, comes from the British Isles. Here at the end of the twelfth century GIRALDUS CAMBRENSIS mentions a long-standing practice of popular part-singing, transmitted from father to son, in Wales and northern England and considers that it was transplanted there from Denmark and Norway. Further, for the first time we meet in the Celtic crwth with a bowed string instrument (already attested in 609) the essence of which is the simultaneous sound of one string bringing out the melody against the harmony of the drone strings. Performance on this instrument must have led quite early to a selection of the more attractive harmonies. Akin to the crwth were various other instruments — the most perfect was the vielle — which maintained their hold on popular favour throughout the Middle Ages. The members of the viol family were their heirs, and the modern violin their grandchild.

The development of polyphony depended in large measure on the theoretical writings of the churchmen. Or, perhaps one might say, the higher culture of the period continually acquired fresh stimulus from sources unknown to us and developed that stimulus still further on its own lines. Frequently the source is still traceable, as in the famous canon *Sumer is icumen in* by the Monk of Reading[?] (*circa* 1300), the monument of a folk-art of unforced imitation, of which the continuation does not appear till half a century later. It may be a mere chance that in the widespread development along similar lines, first France, then Italy, then suddenly England again came to the fore, till in the middle of the fifteenth century the " Netherlanders " (northern French, Flemish, and German composers are included under this name) assumed an undisputed world-power in music.

The first application of theory to polyphony is

the famous description of " organum " in the treatise entitled *Musica Enchiriadis*, which was for long attributed to HUCBALD (*c*. 840–930). This seems to indicate that both in the North and in the South an actual practice — the improvisation of a higher subsidiary part to a given melody — had become stereotyped into a rigid theoretical formula; that is, the addition of one or more subsidiary parts to a liturgical melody at distances of a perfect fourth and fifth. The same treatise, however, also gives instruction in another kind of polyphony, known as " free organum," in which the added part does not follow the given melody in strictly parallel motion. We find polyphony also described by the Greek word " diaphony " and later by its Latin equivalent, " discantus."

In the course of time simple descant, which was unwilling to move more than a fifth away from the " cantus firmus " (as the principal melody was called), very soon learned to assign to the interval of a third the place which theoretical harmony still denied it, and came to realize the value of contrary motion as well as the parallel movement of the parts. The English gymel in two or three parts, which later crossed over to the Continent as fauxbourdon, corresponded to the French practice of " déchant " cultivated at Notre Dame in Paris. It was a form of improvisation, in which the subsidiary parts moved in parallel thirds and sixths with the "cantus firmus."

It is astonishing that, in spite of the improvisatory character of this church music written for voices only, a considerable number of actual records should have survived. Thus from the eleventh century, at the end of which music took a great step forward in France, we have the so-called Winchester Tropes, containing over a hundred and fifty "organa" or pieces for the Mass and the Office, which are characteristically written still in neumes, so that the intervals between the parts are not clear. But manuscripts in line notation dating from the twelfth century give us examples of note-against-note compositions in which the duplum, or upper part, already has a more independent movement. From this it is only a step to the work of the Paris school of Notre Dame, the principal record of which is a manuscript at Florence dating from the middle of the thirteenth century.

At the end of the twelfth century Paris became the main centre for polyphonic music. Here we meet already the names of two typical composers: the elder, Maître Léonin (after 1150), and the younger, Pérotin "le Grand," who reached the height of his creative activity about 1220. In mentioning these names we should remember that the position occupied by musicians in the Middle Ages was fundamentally different from that of the modern "artist." The mediæval musician's life was bounded by the culture of the Church. This was the circle in which he moved and worked; and only if he was a man of genuinely creative gifts did he rise from the position of an anonymous craftsman to the full glory of independence and fame. Léonin worked at his organa as a goldsmith at some fine ornament. He produced a cycle of compositions for the whole of the Church's year, including responses, graduals, and alleluias in the polyphonic style (he did not touch the rest of the liturgy), and called his work or allowed it to be called *Magnus Liber organi de graduali et antiphonario*. For the first time we have a strong contrast between the rigid plainsong tenor and the decorative melismata that move above it. In fact, the upper part has driven the tenor into comparative obscurity in the background. The "descant" parts of this *Magnus Liber* were remodelled by Pérotin; he shortened or expanded them, introduced further melodic elaboration, and gave the upper parts a livelier and more "worldly" character. But much of it he left unaltered; he had no interest in the production of an individual work of art. Three- and four-part organa by him have also been preserved.

All these forms belong to the most primitive stage of polyphony; but it was not long before improvisation was accompanied by the appearance of a further development in the art. This may be called "polymelody," the compulsory combination of two or more distinct melodies with different rhythms and, indeed — what was a most remarkable custom — with texts that were not only different but actually in different languages. The root of this remarkable custom lay in the importance of the trope, so significant a feature of the spirit and art of the Middle Ages. In the past the trope had been merely an interpolation in the liturgical chant; but from the twelfth century it was used as a subsidiary part above the liturgical theme in the tenor, to which it supplied an appropriate interpretation, the two parts being heard simultaneously. Such a combination of several melodies naturally became possible only when the principle of time had previously been established and the nature of consonance and dissonance understood. Among the theorists who accomplished this task was the famous FRANCO OF COLOGNE, who perfected the principle of triple time. The principal form of this primitive yet artistic "polymelody" was the motet, which in some cases combined one or even several secular songs with a liturgical tenor. " Motet " was the name given to the part with a new text over the given tenor; over the motet a third part might be placed (triplum), over that a fourth (quadruplum). But in the thirteenth century the favourite practice was to rest content with the triplum; a fragment of plainsong served as a bass, presumably for instruments, and with this were combined two church paraphrases or, more often, two secular songs with French texts.

The decisive step from organum to the motet was marked by the textual, as also the musical, independence of the upper part, or duplum. This accounts for the term "motet," the text of the upper part being an extension of the "mot" of the tenor. The real difference between a three-part organum and a three-part motet is that in the former the two upper parts are twin melodies, while in the motet the triplum is independent of its companion. There is little question here of free composition, of "creation" in the modern sense of the word; it is an art rather of combination, and this is evident from the numerous ways in which melodies could be combined, as shown in the manuscripts that have been preserved. The same tenor is often accompanied by several dupla, and the same duplum by different tripla. Invention had no part in the spirit of the Middle Ages. The given material was treated with protective care and reverence; it could be used, but not rejected. As Friedrich Ludwig says, "the repertory of tenors used in the *Magnus Liber* remained for a long time practically the only source for the tenors of the French motets." The most curious feature of this form of polyphony was the ingenuous combination of sacred and secular, of liturgical and profane, the arbitrary union — as it seems to us — of incompatible elements. This practice is the result of the fact — noticeable quite early in the motet — that less and less notice was taken of the connexion between the texts of the tenor and duplum. This cheerful unconcern grew until it reached the point where an actual delight was taken in bringing together the most violent contrasts in a single piece. How did this come about? The answer is that in the meantime a secular art, an art of the laity, had been developed to the highest degree of independence, and the church and monastery were no longer the only places where music was cultivated.

From the eleventh century there had existed side by side with the Gregorian chant a secular art of song belonging to the upper classes of civilized society — the art of the Provençal troubadours and the northern French trouvères. Poetry and music were here fused in an inseparable unity. In spirit their art derived from the popular music of the wandering minstrels (descendants of the mimes and "histriones" of the Roman Empire), and the ideals of the period of the Crusades supplied it with new sources of inspiration; but it borrowed its actual form from the monastic sequence. Of the monasteries that cultivated the trope and sequence with loving care and made possible the communication of their treasures to secular art, the most important, apart from St. Gall, was ST. MARTIAL DE LIMOGES; and it was from the neighbourhood of Limoges that the first and most distinguished of the troubadours came. The art of the troubadours began originally with religious stanzas and then turned to subjects and forms of expression which stirred the lofty temper and knightly fancy of the nobles: courtly love, politics and morals (in the "sirventes"), dialogues of the most diverse kinds ("tensos"), disputations (the "jeu-parti"), laments for the death of a nobleman, topical songs, and finally the form related to the sequence — the "lai." Beside this repertory for the castle there grew up that for the village: dances and maying-songs ("estampidos"), rondeaux and pastourelles. The epics ("chansons de geste") belong to both spheres.

Just as the germ of the sacred drama lay in the antiphonal scheme of the sequence and in the trope, as soon as it lighted on the appropriate material — such as the conversation of the three Marys hastening to the tomb, the drama of the Wise and Foolish Virgins, and the Daniel story — so the secular drama developed out of the dance-song. These first dramatic pastourelles display their folk-character in that they are seldom without some sarcastic reference to the courtly classes. To the jongleur fell the task of presenting the music, of giving formal shape to the tunes which his master invented; and it is extraordinary how successful he was in finding the musical solution of the problems of form presented by the varied, elaborately organized, and even over-refined strophic structure of the poet, and with what subtlety he observed the construction of the strophe, the indications of rhyme, the repetitions of part of the strophe, and the relation of the strophe to the refrain.

The text of a large number of songs by the Provençal poets, the troubadours, has been preserved, but unfortunately only a few — just over 250 — of the melodies have survived. Those of the most famous of them, BERTRAN DE BORN, have practically all disappeared. We are much more fortunate with the melodies of the trouvères, of which we possess several hundred, in many cases more than one tune to the same poem. Four generations of trouvères are reckoned during the period from the end of the twelfth to the end of the thirteenth century. COUNT THIBAUT of Champagne, King of Navarre, was the most prolific representative of the third generation; in the fourth we can see the first signs of the change from the aristocracy to the middle classes.

Unlike Provence and northern France, Spain and Italy produced practically nothing but single-voice settings of poems of a sacred or spiritual character. In Spain the principal and indeed almost the only work of this kind is the song-cycle in praise of the Virgin written by King ALFONSO X, OF CASTILE, surnamed "el Sabio" (the Wise), who reigned from 1252 to 1284, and provided with a number of older melodies which, according to Spanish scholars, are derived from Mauro-Andalusian dances. In Italy a new type of sacred song owed its origin to the influence of that great saint FRANCIS OF ASSISI (1182–1226), who was canonized two years after his death. The extent of his influence may be realized by remembering that fifty years after his first foundation there were already eight thousand Franciscan houses all over Europe. This amazing man broke down the Church's privileged right to sing God's praises and enabled the laity to create their own hymns. A new source of inspired popular religious song came into existence — the " laude," congregational hymns for domestic devotions, flagellants' pilgrimages and processions, the melodies of which scarcely changed their character at all until the beginning of the seventeenth century. Before long these hymns adopted dialogue form and so eventually gave birth to the later oratorio; but until about 1400 they remained strictly single-voice settings.

As at the height of the courtly art the jongleur played the most important part in the discovery of the musical side of it, so after its decay the ballad-singer or mendicant musician was active in the dissemination of the secular music of the Middle Ages. Thence proceeded that treasure of song-melody which, side by side with the Gregorian chant, but approximating more nearly by a natural growth to our major and minor tonalities, became the melodic kernel of all the ecclesiastical and secular music of the following centuries. The tensos and sirventes of the trouvères, together with the topical songs of the German Minnesänger, entered on their long winter sleep in the miniature-bedecked manuscripts, while popular tunes were beginning to permeate the whole of polyphonic music with a living force.

The melodies of the Minnesänger were first noted down at a time when they were no longer to be heard from the lips of their creators. Of all the great collections of songs mentioned in histories of literature, only two contain melodies; the first is the Jena Manuscript, dating from the end of the fourteenth century, which contains 91 tunes, and the second, the so-called "Colmar" Manuscript, which has 107 — making a total of 196 (two being common to both collections). There are also a few further pieces, the most beautiful of which are those by the popular singer NEIDHART VON REUENTHAL. In the songs by the Monk of Salzburg, contained in the Mondsee-Wiener Manuscript, there are already some bits of rude polyphony. Only a few decades ago the discovery of the "Münster fragment" gave us a few more melodies by WALTHER VON DER VOGELWEIDE, the finest German song-writer of the Middle Ages. A late follower of the Minnesänger was the South Tyrolese composer COUNT OSWALD VON WOLKEN-STEIN (d. 1445), who also made some experiments in part-writing.

37

The middle-class art of the Meistersinger, a survival of the " Minnegesang," continued for a longer period as a thing worthy of respect but always becoming spiritually drier and musically impotent, a mixture of devotional and secular song but not an organic compound. In these songs the relationship between word and sound, between text and melody, became changed. New texts were written to given melodies; but the tunes themselves were often prolonged to such an impossible length with a mass of ornaments — "Blumen" (flowers), as they were called — that it is very difficult to recognize their original shape, and the poems were limited to didactic and moralizing themes. However, among the many schools of South and central Germany there were one or two prominent Meistersinger who are not to be despised as melodists, such as the Swabian weaver MICHEL BEHEIM in the fifteenth century and the Nuremberg shoemaker-poet HANS SACHS in the sixteenth. The richest collection of Meistersinger tunes (334 " Tone " or tones) is preserved in Adam Puschmann's great song-book, dating from 1584.

It is no mere coincidence that among the motet-composers of the thirteenth century we find a few trouvères, one of whom, ADAM DE LA HALE, became with his *Jeu de Robin et de Marion* the ancestor of all dramatic poet-composers. The motet, originally an embellishment of divine service, but forgetting more and more the consideration of that purpose, pursued a course further and further in the direction of secularity. The liturgical tenors were replaced by secular song-tunes or, at all events, were converted into merely instrumental basses. When in the year 1324 a papal bull laid down stringent regulations against the increasing misuse of polyphony in the Church, the "New Art" was based almost entirely on a middle-class secularity, and continued so for a long time, at least in Italy. "Ars nova" was the name taken by the music of the early fourteenth century in contrast to "Ars antiqua," the motet style of the previous century, principally because it added the doctrine of duple time to the triple time which the "Ars antiqua" regarded as the only road to salvation, and at the same time brought about an extraordinary refinement of notation — the development of an abstract theory of time-measurement, which finally freed polyphony from dependence on a text, and hence on the singing voice, and gave it wings of its own. With the "Ars nova" arrived the possibility of an independent polyphonic instrumental art.

The name "Ars nova" was given to this new art about 1325 by the Bishop of Meaux, Philippe de Vitry (1291–1361), well known as a musician and poet, who also began to strike out new paths as a "composer." The most remarkable evidence of the change in notation is furnished by the celebrated

Montpellier Manuscript. This contains a collection of motets, examples of the old and of the new style being preserved in separate sections; so that in the same manuscript we find both the old or modal notation and also the new or mensural; here the change from the quadrangular to mensural notation is quite plainly marked. There now began a time of endless confusion in notation, which was not cleared up till nearly a century later. About the time of Dante's prime (*c.* 1300), when the Western world received through him its first great poetry in the vernacular, there arose in PIERRE DE LA CROIX of Amiens the first man to make a modest attempt at establishing a new system of rhythm by inventing the smaller note-values. The contrast between long and short notes became more sharply defined as the difference between them became greater, and the vocal character of the art of polyphony changed in favour of the possibilities and tendencies of an instrumental style. The whole art became "humanized." It escaped from the narrow bondage of the Church; the gradual replacement of Latin by French tenors is one of the signs of change. Creative personality made its appearance on an entirely new level of individual craftsmanship. North of the Alps the fourteenth century was the age of GUILLAUME DE MACHAUT, south of the Apennines that of FRANCESCO LANDINO.

Machaut was born in Champagne. He was for many years in the service of the warrior King John of Bohemia and later enjoyed the patronage of the French court. He also became canon of Reims, a post which he held till his death in 1377, honoured and respected as a spiritual leader of his time. He was one of the first of the artist-musicians of the pre-Renaissance period. Even he did not achieve complete freedom in creation; but he worked up his lais, motets, and Masses to the highest pitch of artistry and complexity, showing extraordinary rhythmic subtlety in the use of syncopation, his favourite device, and in his " ballades " — the term includes rondeaux and virelais — he produced a genuine artistic creation, in which at least one subsidiary part was freely invented above a given melody. The " ballade " was an ingeniously constructed song or duet of one or more verses, with one or two supporting or purely ornamental free parts. For well over a century it remained the favourite musical form throughout the Western world. The elaborate artifice of the music had its counterpart in the courtly compliments of the text and the ostentatious splendour of the language, full of learned mythological allusions. Machaut's claim that the ear should be used to check a completed composition was the first indication that the combination of given melodies, the distinguishing characteristic of the old motet style, was beginning to yield to a freer, more individual attitude towards creative art.

In Italy even more than in France the new style

of notation was the sign of a spiritual awakening. The music of the early Renaissance, which centred in northern Italy, and Florence in particular, coincided with the first great flights of Italian poetry of the generation after Dante — the work of Boccaccio and Petrarch — and occupied a corresponding position in musical history. In place of the stiffness of tonality characteristic of the " Ars antiqua " there appeared a finer perception of the possibilities of modulation. In place of the old insensitiveness to faults of part-writing there came a purer style, to which the theorists gave their support by forbidding parallel fifths, unisons, and octaves. For the first time there appeared a free art for the delight of a receptive public, who appreciated and honoured it as art and gave it its place in the culture of civilized society. A surprising abundance of musical forms was suddenly made evident, and a new conception of artistic unity drove the motet style into the background. Composers returned once more with particular pleasure to two-part writing; but at the same time they began to contrive new and more individual settings to fit the stanzas of contemporary poetry, such as the madrigal and the ballata, and whether the tune was in the upper or the lower part it was cunningly embellished with a whole host of *fioriture*. The form was made still more elaborate and complex by the addition of preludes, interludes, and postludes for all manner of instruments. Side by side

with this more refined art song came the resurrec-
tion of the old popular " rota " in an immensely improved form as the " caccia," a canon for two voices
over an original instrumental bass. The form took
the name " caccia " from its text, which originally
presented a hunting-scene or at any rate some lively
incident. Such pieces were the first examples and the
precursors of a long line of vocal program music.

The removal — at once voluntary and involuntary — of the papal court from Rome to Avignon
was symbolical of a change in music. Italian art continued at first dependent on the Paris model, and the
south of France bridged the gulf between the more
mature work of the French composers and the ver-
nal music of Italy. But about the middle of the fourteenth century Italy broke free from this dependence — only, it is true, to relapse into it again
completely at the end of the century. On both sides
of the Apennines, in northern Italy and in Florence,
from about 1340 there were active a whole series of
minor composers — the earliest names being those of
GIOVANNI DA CASCIA and JACOPO DI BOLOGNA — every
one of whom had individuality in a greater or lesser
degree. At the head of all these comes FRANCESCO
LANDINO, the blind organist of San Lorenzo in Florence (d. 1397), master of all instruments of the time,
who was crowned king of poets or musicians at
Venice in 1364. To see an immediate reflection in
literature of the influence of his art, one should read

Giovanni da Prato's *Paradiso degli Alberti* or the stories in Boccaccio's *Decamerone*. His likeness has been preserved on his tombstone in San Lorenzo, where he is represented with his little portable organ, still at that time primarily a secular instrument. Poetry and music both reached a new and glorious level of achievement. A large number of the works of the Italian "Ars nova" have come down to us in the so-called Squarcialupi Manuscript in the Laurenziana at Florence, written in the first quarter of the fifteenth century after the fading of this "proto-Renaissance" or forerunner of the Renaissance proper.

With this provision of new forms, added to the old forms of the conductus and the simpler syllabic composition of polyphonic works, music managed for nearly two hundred years, giving preference now to the one, now to the other, according to the end in view, and learned to handle them, within its limitations, with greater freedom and dexterity. The limitations must not be forgotten. The essence of the art of the fourteenth and fifteenth centuries lay in the subordination of accompanying parts, generally for instruments and richly ornamented, to a single principal part (rarely more than one) which was sung and conformed closely to a song-text, whether sacred or secular; this principal part was the tenor. Composers were still confined to the "horizontal" conception of music, and harmony was the chance result of the movement of the parts. But it is quite clear that in this music we are faced with an alliance of vocal and instrumental elements abundantly rich in possibilities, however uncertain we may be about the interpretation of details. The advance of the fifteenth century on the artistic standard of the fourteenth was many-sided and far-reaching. There was the increase in the number of parts to a normal three or four. Composers showed an increasing delight in displaying their melodic creative gifts by the addition of new and different parts to existing compositions. Then what had been free accompanying parts were themselves placed in the tenor as the basis of new compositions, and composers delighted to show their mutual esteem by such borrowings. Moreover the style of the art song with instrumental accompaniment, as it thrived and blossomed under the care lavished on it, reacted on the composition of music for the Church. The hymn, the motet, parts of the Mass, and ultimately the Mass as a whole were subjected to a polyphonic treatment in which the Gregorian melodies were enveloped in a rich instrumental vesture of accompanying parts and added counterpoints. The need was soon felt to divide up the Mass by changing the number of voices used in its several sections, while at the same time it was considered essential to combine these sections into an artistic whole through the unity of the tenor or the uniformity of themes in the

45

upper parts. Both in sacred and secular music of this century we note the increasing habit of developing the subsidiary parts from themes of the principal part, so as to link them together intellectually, to establish artistic unity not merely by simultaneous combination as in the old motet, but also in the succession of motives. In the rise of a free type of imitation lay the greatest achievement of this century; so great was the enthusiasm with which it cultivated strict canonic writing and made it its boast to move with the highest skill under the greatest restraint.

With regard to the incorporation of the secular style into church music, a distinction must be kept between the forms of the motet (or hymn) and of the separate sections of the Mass and the composition of the Mass as a whole. Even in the fifteenth-century motets there were both old and modern types. The old type was still linked up with the early motet of the previous century, which comprised more than one text; it would introduce, for instance, a second text, with allusions to the particular church festival, to be sung at the same time as the liturgical text, the whole being accompanied by one or two additional instrumental or vocal parts. It was this type of motet that the musicians of the time favoured for occasions of very special importance; an example is the work written by ANTONIUS ROMANUS for the enthronement of Doge Tomaso

46

Mocenigo in 1413, a show-piece of the greatest solemnity and magnificence, combining both the ecclesiastical and the secular styles. In the modern
type of motet, on the other hand, the dominant role
was allotted to one principal part, to which the accompanying parts — usually two lower ones — remained subservient. But with all this subservience
there was a close similarity of character between the
parts. It was as if the old faux-bourdon were coming
to life again in a higher and more artistically conscious sphere of activity. This does not, however,
alter the fact that fifteenth-century music was a simpler art, less subjective and more popular in character than that of the fourteenth century.

Isolated sections of the Mass were also treated in
the same way as the motets. The principal source of
the music of this time — the celebrated Trent
Manuscripts, which were originally in the cathedral
there and later in Vienna and have been in the possession of the Italians since 1919, and which contain
in all about 1600 works by French, Burgundian,
and Flemish composers — consists principally of
such isolated portions of the " Ordo Missæ." Usually the plainsong-melody lies in the upper part,
but it is so obscured by ornaments, appoggiaturas,
and alterations of rhythm, so individualized and
" coloured," that it is by no means easy to distinguish the essential melody. The " accompaniment "
to this part derives from its melodic inflexions, and

there are all sorts of manipulations, both simple and ingenious, of the subsidiary parts.

Among complete, connected settings of the whole of the Mass, which are still rare in the middle of the century, the greater number also have an ornamented liturgical upper part; but all the sections employ a more or less uniform principal theme, which serves as an emblem of the relationship between them. Side by side, however, with this so-called Descant Mass the Tenor Mass was already beginning to emerge. The Tenor Mass holds the texture of the parts together from within, as it were, and to this end uses a liturgical, or more rarely a secular, melody that is generally free from ornamentation, and repeats this melody, often with severe rhythmical modifications, for each section of the Mass. No one troubled very much about whether the tunes had an ecclesiastical flavour. This time of change and unrest, this period of transition from the Middle Ages into modern times, this century at the close of which America was discovered, which was still hesitating between mysticism and humanism, did not distinguish very exactly between ecclesiastical and secular. The appropriation of secular tunes — one of which, *L'Homme armé*, was used by nearly every important musician of the day — went on for over a century and could not be entirely eradicated even by the strict spirit of the

48

Counter-Reformation, which found expression in the resolutions of the Council of Trent.

The external history of this development is that of a great artistic achievement, which seems to have started in England at the beginning of the fifteenth century and is associated with the famous name of John Dunstable. His pupil Binchois carried the impulse to the Continent; but Guillaume Dufay, likewise a pupil of Dunstable, bears the greatest name among composers of the time. With him and his followers, Ockeghem, Obrecht, and many others, began the unique pre-eminence of the Netherland School. With Josquin Després's larger personality the movement reached its summit and was carried indeed over the summit into new artistic territory. Singers and composers from the Netherlands, not only in the churches of their fatherland but also in Paris, Burgundy, Rome, and Naples, held the monopoly of artistic composition. In Spain and northern Italy they drove a national art of song, modest but full of promise for the future, completely into the background, though it is true that they occasionally took an active interest in it themselves. Only in Germany was their influence less active; and although for this reason Germany remained a good way behind the advance of the time and did not reach the climax of its mediæval artistic development till the middle of the sixteenth cen-

tury, German composers were none the less distinguished from the international art of the period by
quite definite characteristics of style in organ music
(KONRAD PAUMANN) and in hymns and motets
(ADAM VON FULDA), by the purity of their melodic
style, by the struggle for vital expression and richness of instrumental tone, and by their aversion to
the use of mere artifice for its own sake.

One of the theoretical writers of the close of the
fifteenth century — indeed, the most important of
them all — the Netherlander JOHANNES TINCTORIS
(1435 or 1436–1511), who worked at the court of
Ferdinand of Aragon in Naples and to whom we owe
the first æsthetic and historical judgments and the
first little dictionary of musical terms, has recorded
the historical fact of the origin of this movement in
England. Another proof, still extant, is the so-called
Old Hall Manuscript, which contains 138 compositions entirely by English musicians. JOHN DUN-
STABLE (c. 1370–1453) was the first to treat a given
"cantus firmus" with free ornamentation and to
put a free and simple accompaniment to it. A sort of
return to the old Celtic pentatonic gave his work a
new power and popular appeal. His two pupils
Binchois and Dufay carried his art to the Kingdom
of Burgundy, which lay between France and Germany and was destroyed before the end of the fifteenth century; this land was of great cultural importance in the formation of social standards, in its

conceptions of chivalry and love, and in all the cere-
monial of court and city. The Emperor Maximilian I
was a later romantic heir of all these ideals. For this
aristocratic and middle-class society GILLES BIN-
CHOIS, who was born about 1400 at Bins or Mons in
Hainault, was *maestro di cappella* and chaplain at
the court of Philippe le Bon, and died in 1460 at
Lille, wrote his fifty-odd songs, beside which his
church music is of quite minor importance. They
are astonishingly sensitive and delicate songs —
gently moving voice-parts with two instrumental
tenors, songs of farewell and other love-songs in
strophic form, which had a particularly strong influence on South German song-writing — an influence which was still effective at the beginning of the
sixteenth century. GUILLAUME DUFAY was a much
more universal type, one of those composers who
represent a whole century. He was born some time
before 1400, probably at Chimay in Hainault,
worked intermittently in the papal chapel, and died
in 1474, a canon at Cambrai. Dufay's compositions
include every type of music of that time, from
chansons and motets of every description to settings of the complete Mass. In the elegance, polish,
sonority, and general character of his style he embraces all the national elements of his time. He is
French in his chansons, Nordic to a striking extent
in his motets and Masses, Italian in the grace that
informs all that he touches. Like Lassus a hundred

years later, he is one of the great international figures of music.

These three, Dunstable, Binchois, and Dufay, are
commonly grouped together under the title of the
" first Netherland school." If this be accepted, we
must also admit a second Netherland school, in
which a list of important composers is headed by
JOHANNES OCKEGHEM, perhaps the most individual
and at any rate the most imaginative of Dufay's
pupils. He was *maestro di cappella* and chaplain to
Charles VII in Paris, and died in 1495 at Tours,
where he was treasurer of the Abbey of St. Martin.
He is the great master of the Mass. We have no
fewer than seventeen Masses by him, besides motets
and a few chansons. He must be regarded as the
chief exponent of the peculiar craftsmanship of the
Netherland school, which consisted in a preference
for canonic writing and the taste for developing
from a single melody a polyphonic movement according to prescribed rules (often expressed in the
form of a riddle) by placing several different time-
signatures at the beginning — a taste that would
seem to prefer ingenuity of construction to vital
expression or a wealth of melodic invention. Undoubtedly, too, mystical signs and purposes play a
part in this sort of craftsmanship; music becomes an
edifice of sound, as for example in Ockeghem's
Deo gratias for thirty-six voices, which is in canon
throughout. With JACOB OBRECHT (b. at Utrecht in

1430, d. at Ferrara in 1505), the most important composer of the third Netherland school, who worked at Cambrai, Bruges, and Antwerp and in Italy, this art of construction grew less complex under Southern influence. Obrecht began as an exponent of "linear counterpoint," but gradually changed to a style of writing in which the texture was clearer and the harmonic basis well defined. His large output numbers twenty-four Masses, twenty-two motets, a *St. Matthew Passion* for several voices, and a quantity of secular works; his influence was enormous.

JOSQUIN DESPRÉS was probably born in Hainault about 1450. He is known to have been a singer in the chapel at the court of the Sforzas at Milan, in the Vatican chapel at Rome, and at Cambrai, Modena, possibly Paris, and Ferrara. He died in 1521, a prebendary of Condé. Like Claudio Monteverdi in the seventeenth century, he summed up all the achievements of the fifteenth century and, filling them with new meaning, transmitted them to the sixteenth. His work — thirty Masses, many motets and chansons — remained the model for his generation and that which followed it; and so great was his importance that no musician of his day could remain unaffected by it. He increased the number of parts to six and employed all the constructive skill and craftsmanship of the fifteenth century, not so much for its own sake as to impart an entirely individual

expression to it. Not that his music is an illustration
of the text; but he seizes the spirit of his subject —
earnest, tender, solemn, or majestic — with a passionate precision. In him was attained the ideal of
"Gothic" church music — universal in style and
yet a personal creation. And if we take into account
his contemporaries as well — the pensive and gentle
PIERRE DE LA RUE, the genial ANTOINE BRUMEL, the
brilliant LOYSET COMPÈRE, and many others — the
high water-mark of genuine church music would
seem to be, not in Palestrina's day, but already at
this time, on the threshold of the Renaissance.

Of the German composers who from the modest
beginnings of an indigenous polyphonic style of
song-composition — the principal source of this
music being the *Locheimer Liederbuch*, compiled
after the middle of the century — came to throw in
their lot with the "international" music of the
Netherland school, only two need be mentioned:
HEINRICH ISAAK and ALEXANDER AGRICOLA. Isaak
was actually of Flemish origin, and through his activity in Italy — at Ferrara and Florence — and his
extensive travels was one of the most "international" composers of the time. But he was a German
none the less; and that not merely on account of his
service at the court of Archduke Sigismund at Innsbruck and in the many households of the Emperor
Maximilian — at Augsburg, Vienna, and Constance
— but also by reason of his natural inclinations. He

died in 1517 at Florence. He is at home in all styles — in Italian songs, chansons, Masses, and in his great cycle of motets, the *Choralis Constantinus*, written for the cathedral at Constance. But he is most himself in German song. His song of farewell, *Innsbruck ich muss dich lassen*, with its individual melody in the upper part, was, in spite of its modest scope, an epoch-making piece of music, just as Mozart's *Veilchen* was two hundred and fifty years later. Alexander Agricola also travelled much. He was *maestro di cappella* at Milan, Cambrai, Mantua (with the Gonzagas), and finally at the court of Philippe le Beau in Burgundy, in whose service he died at Valladolid, probably in 1506. He, too, exerted an international influence with his Masses, chansons, and Italian songs.

This international influence was made possible by the invention of music-printing about 1500. This produced as great a revolution in the history of music as book-printing had done in the history of general European culture. A quarter of a century after Gutenberg's first attempts, German and Italian printers produced printed missals. The decisive step — the printing of the notation of measured music from type — was taken by Ottaviano dei Petrucci of Fossombrone, who worked at Venice and in his native town. His editions of Masses, motets, chansons, and " frottole " put all later examples out of the running by their perfection. Venice, following his example, remained the principal centre for the printing and publishing of polyphonic music. But this "black art" also spread throughout Europe with amazing rapidity, and nowhere more so than in Germany and France.

THE "RENAISSANCE"

New Forms

IT is tempting to maintain that the sixteenth century was more than any other period in the development of music a time of transition — a time spent in putting the finishing touches to what had already been done and in preparing the ground for what was yet to come. We find two streams flowing side by side, one ebbing, the other rising; between them there are connexions, both seen and unseen, which give the music of this century its peculiar brilliance and dazzling contrasts. The taste of the last years of the

Middle Ages was all in favour of strict imitation, the cultivation of the canon in the simplest and most recondite forms of inversion, diminution, and augmentation. The mediæval ideal of music based on construction was magnificently realized in the sixteenth century, particularly in the composition of Masses and motets. It is true that certain technical tricks of the preceding period, such as the development of a polyphonic work from a single part, were abandoned. But in strictness of composition and genuine craftsmanship there are a large number of Masses and motets of the sixteenth century that are in no way inferior to the technical achievements of men like Ockeghem and Obrecht. Indeed, this art of ingenious and skilful combination enjoyed an astonishing new lease of life at the end of this century and the beginning of the next.

But at the same time a completely new spirit pervades the music of the sixteenth century. The chief sign of this is a change in the relationship between the vocal and instrumental elements in a musical composition, between the chief melody and the accompanying parts. The period up to about 1520 may be characterized as that of rich and varied cultivation of song accompanied by voices or instruments. But from now on, the general structure of vocal composition was controlled by instrumental principles, though the individual constituents were motifs following vocal laws and inspired by poetic fancies. In this way the shape of the new motet and madrigal originated. These forms show that a totally new conception of the unity of a work of art had once more been arrived at, a new sense of relationship between superior and subordinate elements. The old unity of calculated construction was succeeded by a new poetic unity, resulting from the free play of the artist's imagination. A work no longer depended on a given melody running through it to hold it together; the composer shaped and unified it, as it were, with his own hands. For the first time he employed contrast freely, as his text demanded, between homophony and imitation and between few and many voice-parts. Especially in the working of motifs in free imitation he now gained a wonderfully delicate instrument of expression. The music of the fifteenth century had been full of ingenuity and intellectual contrivance; what the sixteenth century contributed was the directly sensuous, poetic expression of an idea. We find these two attitudes most wonderfully reconciled in Bach, who may be said in this sense to have succeeded to an artistic inheritance that was centuries old.

Throughout the century the motet forms the enthralling scene of conflict between the old and new tendencies. There were several subdivisions of the form, treated in a more or less conservative or progressive style — the psalm-settings fall into the latter category — and of its composers some inclined to

old, others to new methods, one of the most impetuous being Orlandus Lassus. But the true outlet for
the advanced movement, the arena for all innova-
tion and experiment, was the madrigal, in which all
the possibilities of expression of that age were first
combined. Originating from the fifteenth-century
frottole — small strophic songs, half-serious in character, still for the most part instrumentally accompanied — its musical pattern at first clearly imitated
the form of the sonnet and the canzona. But it did
so with purely vocal means, chiefly, to begin with,
in four-part, preferably homophonic songs. At the
same time it fundamentally changed its tone; it
sought nobility and fastidious refinement to the
point of extravagance and sentimental affectation.
With ADRIAN WILLAERT, however, and especially
with his pupil CIPRIANO DE RORE there began a fuller
development of its resources. Five voices became
the norm, and with this the choral web grew subtler
and richer in colour. Homophonic and imitatively
handled sections alternated; the chorus was cunningly subdivided to throw individual lines of the
poem into relief. Tonality came to be treated more
freely and boldly. Rore initiated a chromaticism
which later, especially in the compositions of LUCA
MARENZIO and GESUALDO DA VENOSA, was to lead
to extremes of daring — but not based upon clear
harmonic perception and hence not fully absorbed
by the main stream of development.

Above all, however, the madrigal brought about a new conception of the motif as a symbol. The composer sought an expression that would exactly match the poem of his choice. The motif was no longer to be a mere garment, so to speak, for the text; it was to be as precisely expressive as the text itself. The laborious efforts of madrigalists in this direction often betrayed them into a naïve tone-painting in which they lost sight of the work as a whole in the detail; but the close observation of nature involved was a step towards true poetic expression. Towards the end of the sixteenth century the madrigal became more and more infused with dramatic life, and this despite the number of its voice-parts and a seemingly inappropriate form. In the numerous dialogues the tendency shows itself conspicuously. Anyone acquainted with the admirable character-studies contained in MONTEVERDI's madrigals, for instance, will realize from them alone that here we are standing on the threshold of modern art. The madrigal is a wonderful product of vital emancipated music, worthy of the Renaissance. Its clear-cut, individualized structure bears witness to the finest social culture. The diversity, the refinement of its expression, the exhaustive development of its resources by its best exponents are unsurpassed and unsurpassable.

So far, that is to say, as the resources of the medium went; but the limitations of that pure a-cappella art render it essentially different in expression from music of later times. Wherein does its strangeness lie? Not so much in the tonality of the madrigalists — for in the trend during the century towards the major and minor modes those progressions of unrelated chords so charming to our ears occurred less and less frequently — as in a wealth of rhythmical effects, the result of their peculiar conception of independent part-writing. And then in their different attitude towards construction and dynamic effects. The age of a-cappella music was certainly not ignorant of accumulative and intensifying devices — at any rate, after part-writing for more than four voices came in, and especially when use was made of multiple choirs — but the art was not yet learned of intensifying by means of the organization of contrasting sections, of that inner musical intensification attained by the dramatically conceived development of a theme or themes. In the language of exaggeration one might say that an a-cappella piece, provided it reached a satisfying length and preserved unity of tonality, could come to an end where it chose. It was this placidity of movement, this perpetual ebb and flow, this seemingly inexhaustible outpouring of melody, that so captivated the Catholic enthusiasts of the romantic movement in the nineteenth century. But towards the close of the sixteenth century came the time for contrasting themes to appear in the madrigal, and

with them the first attempts at structure and cumu-
lative effects in the modern sense.

In the course of the century the leadership of the
world of music passed to Italy, and the process is
clearly to be followed in the history of the madrigal.
In the fifteenth century, at the time when she was
making her way to cultural predominance, Italy
had played a subordinate role in musical art. It is
significant that Lorenzo de' Medici, when he wished
to hear one of his canzones artistically set to music, had to apply through his organist Antonio
Squarcialupi to a Northerner, Guillaume Dufay.
In the first half of the sixteenth century the Netherlands still dominated musical Italy. But as time went
on, the Italians so assimilated the achievements of
the foreigner that by the end of the century they
represented, with the forms they had cultivated
(madrigal, villanella, canzonetta, balletto) and their
vocal (double chorus) and instrumental style (ricercar, canzon francese, toccata), the foremost artistic power of the age and set the standard for
Germany, England, and, to a lesser degree, France.
The later Netherlanders no longer set the fashion
for Italy; they themselves were already under the
siren's spell, which few could resist.

Not that Italy reached this position single-handed.
The brilliant artistic attainments of the century
were only possible, and are only comprehensible,
through the competition of the various musical na-

tions. There was an incessant give-and-take, a perpetual appropriating and remodelling. The international character of art, the interest in foreign
achievements and their ungrudging and swift assimilation — something that later only German music was to carry on, to its prosperity and peril —
never flourished so easily and surely as at that time.
The principal contribution made by the French
was in the form of the chanson — a contribution,
light in content while enormous in bulk, of an airy,
sprightly music, full of pretty babblings and devoted to sentimental love-ditties, with a preference
for a tone of refined *grivoiserie*. A peculiarity of
this literature, which soon came to be imitated
everywhere, was programmatic description by
purely vocal means, in the manner of the old Florentine caccia — of street noises, battle scenes, and
the warbling of birds — in most cases applied to an
onomatopœic text. Through the simplicity and
clarity of its form and themes the chanson, transformed into the canzon francese, greatly influenced
the budding instrumental music. While the ricercar
was the ancestor of the fugue, the chanson was the
soil out of which the sonata was to grow. The
modern variation form seems to have had its original home in Spain. A development similar in many
respects to that of Italy and contemporary with
it took place there, political ties connecting that
country equally with Italy and the Netherlands.

Spain produced a large number of church composers of the highest rank, peculiarly distinguished by
the glowing mysticism of their expression. Here
at an early date the variation form seems to have
originated, based upon a recognition of the harmonic foundations of the theme. We possess lute
variations by Spanish masters of the 1530's, variations for viola da gamba of the year 1553, and keyboard variations of the same period, especially by the
great master Antonio de Cabezon, which do not differ in principle from the achievements of Bach, Beethoven, and Brahms.

Such was the field of art which the teeming composers of the Netherlands, France, England, Germany, Spain, and Italy made amazingly productive.
Among them were figures of the most pronounced
individuality. The representatives of the period,
GIOVANNI PIERLUIGI DA PALESTRINA and ORLANDUS
LASSUS, count among the great men of Western
civilization — Palestrina as the composer of the ideal
type of church music, pure, purged of all subjectivity, marvellously harmonious, Lassus as the most
versatile and vigorously creative master of the motet, madrigal, villanella, and chanson. These two
absorbed and fulfilled the entire musical art of their
age. Palestrina (1525–94), who from 1571 was
maestro di cappella at St. Peter's in Rome, was heir
to all the traditions of his Roman predecessors and
was also steeped in the music of the Netherlanders,

which he transfused into an expression of utter purity and immaculate, unearthly longing. Lassus (1532–94), a Fleming, from 1556 head of the Munich court chapel, found the decisive stimulus for his art in the Italian madrigal. Palestrina was master of the Mass — we possess ninety-three four- to eight-part Masses by him — Lassus of the motet (the huge collection of his motets, *Magnum Opus Musicum*, contains over five hundred examples), as also of the madrigal, villanella, chanson, and German Lied, all of which he mastered like his mother-tongue. The two were as equally great in creative power as they were different in nature. The one commanded a serene flow of music, raising it to supernal heights; the other was full of explosive strength, of dramatic vitality controlled with effort. The one was a lover of songful melisma; the other of vigorous declamation. The one was essentially a church composer (his secular madrigals are of hardly any importance either in his life-work or in the history of the genre); the other in his madrigals the noble singer of love both sensual and super-sensual, in his chansons of sportive *joie de vivre*, and in his villanellas a forerunner of the commedia dell' arte. A veritable Proteus was Lassus, with his power of changing his musical style; indeed, one of the greatest masters of all time in his virile strength, his unconquerable creative urge, his force of expression, his keen sense of the comic.

66

New Forms

While Rome, through Palestrina and his pupils, became more than ever the focus of musical life in Italy, the influence of the powerful Venetian school, through ANDREA and GIOVANNI GABRIELI, uncle and nephew, reached out beyond the frontiers of Italy. Palestrina and Lassus inherited and perfected an art which was nearing its maturity; but with Giovanni Gabrieli music seems to have burst into fresh bloom. At Venice a style of composition for several choirs prevailed, founded by Willaert and cultivated by his successors Rore, Zarlino, Andrea Gabrieli, Donato, and Croce. Instead of single voices, a work was built upon the question and answer, the timbre, the echo, the tonal combination of differently constituted choirs of voices and instruments. Giovanni Gabrieli brought this style to the zenith of its effect. He did more: through a new disposition of vocal and instrumental elements and the invention of a new kind of motif, he led the way into untrodden territory. A personality at once conservative and daring, preserving and augmenting, he avoided the mistake that contemporary and later choral composers committed, of relying on the merely passing effect. His music was brilliant, yet profound; festive, yet for the Church — albeit a specifically Venetian Church; full of power, romance, and wonderfully glowing colour. His *Symphoniæ Sacræ* (1597 and 1615) was the decisive work of a new trend in choral composition.

With the Gabrielis not only was the way paved for a relation between choir and orchestra that was to remain permanently valid; but also the separation of vocal and instrumental music-making was completed. We have noticed already how purely instrumental laws governed the structure of the new musical product of the sixteenth century. Through the transference of vocal pieces to instruments — to the organ and to ensembles of strings and wood-wind — inherently instrumental forms gradually came to detach themselves from the hitherto undifferentiated pattern. Out of the motet, with its various subdivisions, came the ricercar (a fugue with several themes in succession) and the fantasia (a fugue with a single theme), the latter eventually supplanting the ricercar, which was the form more cultivated in the sixteenth century. Out of the chanson the canzon francese, the prototype of the sonata, developed. The most valuable elements that the canzon adopted from its vocal model were the rhythmic precision and animation of its motifs and the lucid harmonic lay-out of its form. Concurrent with this was the development of the instrumental dance, which cultivated a wealth of forms, ceasing more and more to be mere *Gebrauchsmusik*, supplying themes for variations and already at this early period assembling a cycle of dance forms to create the suite. Along with the development of form went the improvement of

68

performance; the pursuit of instrumental style was accompanied by the evolution of the particular technics of the domestic keyboard instruments, of the organ, and of string and wood-wind instruments. The virtuoso appeared, at first on the lute, the favourite instrument of the time. German organ-playing of this time, with its conventional " colourists," had nothing to compare with the Italians' handling of the strict and free forms of ricercar, prelude, and toccata — the solo piece *par excellence* — and still less with the English, whose music for the virginal, in which they especially cultivated variations and the toccata, was a genuine, astonishingly subtle keyboard art. Towards the end of the century the Canzon francese divides (though not always very sharply) into two separate types — the Sonata for wind instruments and the Canzona for strings. The former is a fully scored piece of festal music, the latter chamber music, more lightly scored and more delicately wrought. The one is the ancestor of the symphony and the concerto, the other of the chamber sonata. An important part was played in the whole instrumental art of the sixteenth century by the practice of improvising ornamentation.

For a century and more the Venetian school, with Andrea and Giovanni Gabrieli at its head, exercised a decisive influence on Germany and the Netherlands by their instruction in every branch

of music. Andrea Gabrieli was the teacher of HANS
LEO HASLER and, with Zarlino, of JAN PETERSZOON
SWEELINCK (1562–1621), who in turn was to hand
on the tradition to a whole succession of considerable German musicians. Giovanni Gabrieli's teach-
ing speaks for itself in the fact that HEINRICH
SCHÜTZ was his pupil. But even had he not had many
other pupils, the favourable position of Venice and
the magic of his music would still have induced
German music to follow in the wake of the Bu-
cintoro.

As in a remote little flower-garden, Germany had
until then cultivated her secular song. For long the
technique of the form, deriving from the fifteenth
century and having little in common with the free
methods of the later age, had remained the same.
Following the style of the court song, the words
and tunes of which were kept in circulation by
wandering minstrels, this German secular song presents a more or less artful interweaving of parts,
generally capable of either vocal or instrumental
execution, twining around the melody sung by the
tenor. After the three-part writing of the *Locheimer Liederbuch* these songs were normally composed, at the hey-day of their vogue about 1530,
in four or, at the most, five parts. A simple form,
closely matching that of the verse, was preferred
to the pretentious architecture of the motet. Two-
part counterpoint occurs characteristically, with

graceful cadences, a preference for the Lydian mode, and withal a refined and charming rhythmic pattern calculated to enhance the air. Chiefly they were, of course, love-songs; but some were occupational songs, and sentiments of an edifying, reflective, and also political nature found utterance. A special place was taken by drinking-songs and convivial ditties, the expression of a robust material enjoyment, culminating in the quodlibet, with its innumerable quips and allusions. The scope of this lyricism, ranging from homely heartiness and tenderness to simple grandeur, shows how wide must have been the response it could count upon from the German people and how deep-rooted it was in their hearts. An indication of this is the fact that no composer ever published a collection consisting entirely of his own songs. In contrast to the exclusive and subjective art of the madrigal, these songs represented a sheer gift to the community. They are preserved in a few large anthologies, the most important of which, containing 380 songs, is the five-volume collection (1539–56) of the art-loving physician Georg Forster. Among a large number of more or less unimportant craftsmen the outstanding composers after HEINRICH ISAAK — who, true German that he was, hit the nail straight on the head — were HEINRICH FINCK, THOMAS STOLTZER (d. 1526), PAUL HOFHAIMER, organist to the Emperor Maximilian, and, above all, ARNOLD VON

BRUCK and the Swiss LUDWIG SENFL. The last of these especially was a writer of masterly songs, tender or noble or, again, full of humour. He ranged over the whole gamut of song from the rude and racy to the sublime. The homophonic settings of verses in classical metres by Hofhaimer and Senfl have a curious place of their own beside these songs. The humanistic movement which in Italy urged men to a vigorous creative renewal of the spirit of antiquity took on in Germany the character of pedantry. In the last thirty years of the century the ground where those blossoms had flowered seemed to dry up. Italian influence and actual importations of Italian music had an easy conquest. A number of artists, indeed, attempted to introduce certain ingredients from the South into the home-made brew, now running so thin; but the attempt failed.

Things were different in England. In the past she had given a new impulse to the whole of European music, and she still retained her rightful position beside the other nations. She produced such fine ecclesiastical composers as CHRISTOPHER TYE and ROBERT WHITE and set beside the grand and noble simplicity of the church music of THOMAS TALLIS (d. 1585) the more personal, more subjective, more imaginative art of WILLIAM BYRD (d. 1623), one of the most distinguished composers of the age. In 1588 the Italian madrigal and canzonetta in their maturity crossed the Alps and came to England, where they continued to flourish in English dress for, roughly, thirty years. Composers like MORLEY, WILBYE, and WEELKES gave the madrigal an extraordinary increase of intensity and the canzonetta an added grace. Their music was worthy of the age for which Shakspere wrote. Between 1588 and 1627 more than forty books of madrigals appeared, ranging from Byrd's *Psalms, Sonnets and Songs for five voices* to Hilton's *Airs or Fa-las for three voices*. Among them was Morley's collection *The Triumphs of Oriana* (1601), the title and arrangement of which were a close imitation of the Italian *Trionfo di Dori* (1592). The Italian collection having been dedicated to a Venetian lady, *The Triumphs of Oriana* was published as an act of homage to Queen Elizabeth; it included contributions from twenty-three composers. This close relationship to all the various forms of the later Italian madrigal, from two-part songs to settings for double choir, remained unchanged throughout the work of Byrd, Morley, Weelkes, Wilbye, Farmer, Farnaby, East, Bateson, Lichfield, Pilkington, Tomkins, and Gibbons; and this is equally true of the lyrical madrigal, with its wealth of subjective expression, of the saucy canzonetta, and of the gay and cheerful ballet. Many of the texts were translations of Italian models, but a large number also were characteristic and original poems.

73

It would be a mistake to regard the English madrigal as a mere imitation of its Italian forebear. These English composers did not make "originality" their specific aim, and they were quite ingenuous in the way in which they took over the forms of Gabrieli, Marenzio, and Vecchi. But their music is shot through and through with the spirit of a more abundant, more essential, more virile feeling for melody. Instead of the Italian conventionality and over-refinement of expression we find a more personal spirit, a more robust and more natural emotion, not to mention a greater certainty, instinctively acquired, in the handling of harmony and rhythm. The individuality of all these composers is clearly marked: William Byrd, the greatest artist of them all, for all his severe restraint; Thomas Morley, his pupil, particularly devoted to the light and graceful ballet; Thomas Weelkes, subjective and unequal in achievement; above all, John Wilbye, an inspired composer and master of all the resources of expression, who shows not only the greatest daring but also the most finished taste. The composers of the later generation, such as ORLANDO GIBBONS, JOHN WARD, and THOMAS TOMKINS, used themes and thematic contrasts that already foreshadowed, as in the works of the contemporary Italians, the end of music of this type. At the same time the English madrigal — thanks to the devotion to tradition shown by a few music-lovers — was kept alive for over three centuries, and a direct connexion can be traced between it and the vocal music of England at the present day.

Germany, on the other hand, soon gave up the struggle and preferred to write purely Italian madrigals. The Italian villanella also appeared, first in its own tongue, though it took on a superficially German character when it became a "Bauerliedlein" — superficially, since in Italy the three-part villanella was almost entirely dedicated to parody and could be fully appreciated only within the conventions of, and as a contrast to, an exceedingly sophisticated state of culture. A very curious turn was taken when these songs were adapted to suit "Christian, edifying and moral" sentiments. Later, through the example of Gastoldi and Vecchi, the canzona for several voices (generally five) and the balletto started their triumphant progress through Germany, where they were to enjoy a career far more lasting and influential than in the country of their origin. The balletto found its way into the dance-suite and also brought fresh vigour — again through the example of Vecchi and Banchieri — to the old quodlibet, giving rise to a whole literature of choruses and songs of a folk-character, which, above all in central and southern Germany, succeeded in maintaining its place in the domestic mu-

sic of the country with refreshing vitality and came
to light again at the beginning of the eighteenth
century.

The foreign plant was first really acclimatized
by HANS LEO HASLER of Nuremberg. Not that he
was the first to draw from the wells of Italian art;
but the way in which he absorbed that spirit and
then brought it forth to new life — the way, for
instance, in which in his *Neue deutsche Liedlein*
(1591) he transformed the Italian canzonetta from
a parodistic or pseudo-pastoral form into a choral
song instinct with more sincere feeling and charm —
is a most significant illustration of the relationship
of German music to foreign influences. From this
point of view Hasler was actually the true forerunner — in contrast to the numerous composers
like Hasse and Graun — of Schütz, Handel, and
Mozart.

Among Hasler's works special importance at-
taches to the *Psalmen und christliche Gesänge*
(1607) and the *Kirchengesänge: Psalmen und
geistliche Lieder* (1608). They bear witness to the
measure in which this Italianate musician was attached to that simple yet so significant expression
of the spirit of the German Reformation, the communal song of the Protestant Church — the chorale.
In those stern times the chorale had come to include
practically the whole of German song, secular as
much as religious, and within the narrowest frame-

work had become crystallized into a form as capable of the profoundest symbolism as it was of surviving the wear and tear of generations. In 1523 and 1526 Luther had provided the evangelical service with a new liturgical form which, after having at first been in the hands of the clergy and choir, made room, even in the time of the great reformer himself, for increasing participation by the congregation. Instead of their allotted portions of the Mass, of matins and of vespers, the members of the congregation now sang hymns before and after the sermon and at the end of the service — hymns derived from all manner of sources. Some originated from Gregorian chants, others from pre-Reformation sacred folk-songs, while new sources of secular folk-song were always being drawn upon. Among the most notable appropriations from the secular domain were the psalm-tunes in use in the Calvinistic Church, arranged in four-part harmony by CLAUDE GOUDIMEL from French chanson-melodies and introduced to German congregations in a translation by Ambrosius Lobwasser, a professor at Königsberg (1573).

This priceless treasure of melody was to have an eventful history. In the *Geystliche Gesangkbüchleyn* of JOHANN WALTHER (1524), Luther's musical adviser, and again in *Newe deudsche geistliche Gesenge* by GEORG RHAW (1544) and in other less important works, these melodies are artistically

77

arranged with a view both to domestic devotions and to performance by the trained church choir, with the tune in the tenor according to the contemporary German usage. By the end of the century, however, the tune had made its way into the treble. The artist with his personal feelings had effaced himself behind the symbolic act of congregational prayer. Such a treatment of the chorale as is found in Hasler's *Psalms* (the production of 1607 mentioned above) where the chorale is "*fugweis componiert*" (fugally treated) became the exception. The general rule was to leave the chorale untouched — "*simpliciter gesetzt.*" It is only necessary to recall the highest development of this art — J. S. Bach's chorales — to realize how wide a scope for poetic interpretation was afforded to composers in the harmony and part-writing of this kind of arrangement. The symbolic content of the chorale found its supreme expression in pure instrumental music, in compositions for the organ. Of decisive importance here was the *Tabulatura nova* of the Halle organist SAMUEL SCHEIDT (1624), whose chorale arrangements lead straight to the art of the great Protestant organ school and to the Bach cantata.

Accompanied Monody

Viewed as a whole, the sixteenth century was one of the most extraordinary periods of conflict in the history of music. It is true that, in spite of the open warfare between old and new, in which rival pens played their part, it passed more quietly than similar contentions in later times — those, for example, that raged round Gluck and about the " New German " school. But the conflict was there none the less. From the beginning of the century every composer had to find his own answer to questions that affected his very essence as an artist; he had to resolve in himself the struggle between homophony and polyphony, between the differing claims of vocal and instrumental expression, between melody as the servant of language and as the vehicle for ornament. Only the greatest masters, the composers of all-embracing genius, found it easy to reconcile the conflicting claims and instinctively hit upon the right solution in every branch of music. National divisions were revealed by the different tendencies. The Germans and Netherlanders pursued an ideal of instrumental polyphony, rich in harmonic possibilities — the organ chorale and the fugue — which also had a decisive influence on their

79

vocal writing. The Italians, on the other hand, aimed at perfecting instrumental melody, an ideal that pointed the way to the sonata, the concerto, and the aria. In Haydn's sonata form these various currents were one day to be harmonized and reconciled.

One of the practical evidences of this period of conflict and its actual outcome was music-drama or opera, which appeared in its first rough outlines in the last decade of the sixteenth century. Opera involves the co-operation of several arts and many factors. Its origins, therefore, are many and deeply rooted in the past, and the separate ingredients that conditioned the particular form of the new art are clearly distinguished. This form was determined in the first place by the Italian intermezzo. It was customary in the dramatic performances that took place before the aristocratic audiences of the Italian courts to fill up the entr'actes with dances and scenic representations, generally taken from classical mythology, the aim being to excite wonder and astonishment by a novel and decorative spectacle. Soon, however, there was a change of method. Scenes of this kind began to be enlivened by action and eventually they were combined together into a dramatic whole in much the same way as later, in the eighteenth century, opera buffa developed out of the comic intermezzo. An impetus was given to this development by the allegorical festival-play produced to celebrate some event at court, in which words were indispensable. From another starting-point the masquerade tended in the same direction. Its original form, which for long remained the same, was the carnival song — those licentious stanzas which a small troupe of mummers directed at the ladies who were present at the festival. In the second half of the century the tone of these songs became more refined and there was more variety in the invention. The carnival song began to be treated dramatically and its character became more like that of the intermezzo. Finally, in the course of the century music was used more and more in the choruses and dances of the pastoral drama. This had evolved from dramatic eclogues modelled on those of Theocritus and Virgil. As time went on, its popularity increased so much that it became the delight of the whole age. After Tasso's *Aminta* the masterpiece in this form was Guarini's *Pastor fido*, which was idolized by the fashionable world. It was in the realm of classical mythology and pastoral drama that opera was launched on its career.

In this hybrid dramatic form there had begun to appear quite early, in addition to choruses and dances, solo songs accompanied by a single instrument — lute, lyre, or bass viol — or by more imposing instrumental forces. No one can follow the history of these festival performances in the various capitals — first at Venice and then particularly at

Ferrara under the auspices of the Este family and
at Florence under the Medici — without noticing
how such solo songs borrowed from the forms of
vocal music current at the time — the frottola, the
canzonetta, and, above all, the madrigal in all its
stages of development. Experiments of this kind
brought nearer a problem whose solution was to be
one of the greatest achievements of the Renaissance
— the problem of genuine monody — that is, melody sung by a single voice with instrumental accompaniment. Composers were at first content to
take a madrigal in several parts, which would naturally be polyphonic in conception, and extract a
single part, generally the top one, turning it into a
vocal solo and fitting the other voices underneath
it as instrumental accompanying parts. This solo
voice-part was lavishly ornamented by means of
coloratura. The weakness of this experiment from
the point of view of style was, however, soon realized. It was seen that the isolation of a single part
above the others was arbitrary and artificial, and the
vocal embellishment of the solo was superficial and
inimical to true expression. In the composition of
songs there was a movement towards preserving the
distinctness of the poet's words, and in the drama
towards a faithful interpretation of emotion.

There was in Florence a dilettante circle, composed of amateurs, poets and musicians, who were
inspired by idealistic conceptions of the might and

majesty of classical drama. Here the new movement found a formulation of its theoretical principles and an attempt at their practical realization. The demand that the text should be intelligible was not new. The Church had more than once condemned the impropriety of the simultaneous use of different texts in motets and Masses. We know, too, what importance the Council of Trent assigned not only to the purely moral but also to the æsthetic question. The delegates were anxious that the service of God should not be profaned by the introduction of secular songs; but they were equally insistent that sacred words should have their proper value in polyphonic settings.

The members of the Florentine circle went farther, rejecting polyphony as detrimental to poetry. The struggle against counterpoint, however, was only the negative part of their program. Of their positive endeavour — to achieve true accompanied solo song — the first examples, by VINCENZO GALILEI, have not survived; but we have a number of later attempts, first among them some small-scale lyrical settings by the Roman composer GIULIO CACCINI, published in 1602 under the proud title *Nuove Musiche*. They consist of madrigals and strophic songs composed with a meticulous regard for metrical accuracy. They are not without a certain melodic charm, and the composer, who was himself a singer, was not afraid to introduce vocal ornamentation, although the program of the new school expressly excluded coloratura. The voice-part is supported by a bass of the simplest type, the realization of the harmony being left for the accompanist to improvise. These miniatures were followed in 1597 by JACOPO PERI's *Dafne*, the first drama to be set to music throughout. With the production at Florence in 1600 of two settings of *Euridice* by Caccini and Peri and of Emilio Cavalieri's *Rappresentazione di anima e di corpo*, opera and sacred music-drama made their first public appearance.

The origin of opera in æsthetic principles was a complete contradiction of all the conditions that should attend the birth of a genuine creative work of art; but the Florentine movement nevertheless gave a strong impulse to its growth. This was particularly so in the case of the recitative, with which their arguments were principally concerned. It combined originally the elements of both the declamatory and the lyrical styles; but gradually a separation of the two took place, and the result was the emergence of pure declamation and pure melody — the aria. The other ingredient of the new monody, the basso continuo, seems to have been an assimilation and adaptation of a practice which polyphony had already made its own towards the end of the sixteenth century in another form — the " basso seguente." When works for several voices or several choirs —

particularly those of the Venetian and northern Italian school — were performed, it often happened that there was a lack of sufficient vocal and instrumental resources. The organist then had to help things out by accompanying the whole work in unison with the voices. But this meant that he had to have a complete organ score in tablature before him, the writing of which involved the expenditure of much time and trouble and, considering the enormous amount of music used, was practically out of the question. The necessity for something simpler and the increased understanding of harmony led to the adoption of an abbreviated notation — the mere indication of a continuous bass line, going with whatever happened at any moment to be the lowest part, on which the expert reader built up the whole harmonic superstructure of the work. A simple system of figures written under or above the notes showed the deviations from the root positions of common chords — that is, chords of the sixth and six-four, suspensions, and discords. The adoption of this system, which remained in force for over a hundred and fifty years, was made easier by the choral style of the Venetian school, which was generally homophonic in character. It was the *maestro di cappella* at St. Mark's, Venice, GIOSEFFO ZARLINO, who laid the foundations of modern conceptions of harmony in his *Istituzioni armoniche* and so created a system on which the whole art of continuo-playing depended. In this art the feeling for harmony continued to develop throughout the seventeenth century until it culminated in Bach's miraculous instinct. It has generally been associated with the name of the northern Italian composer LODOVICO GROSSI DA VIADANA, but it was actually much older; it came into existence quite quietly and unobtrusively, and Viadana only put into writing in a clear if still rather primitive manner the rules for accompanying and emphasized the necessity for accepting a limited number of parts as a postulate. In his hundred *Concerti ecclesiastici* for one, two, three, and four voices (1602 and 1608) he supplied a kind of practical manifesto which had an important influence.

The basso continuo radically changed the whole form and shape of musical composition down to its smallest constituents. Along with music in several parts, there was now music in a few parts, in which the voices were brought together in an entirely new relationship, while the bass absorbed, so to speak, what had previously been the middle parts and became in a way an antithesis to the melodic line of the song or the upper parts. By accepting a subordinate and supporting role it set the upper parts free and allowed them to appear in a new guise — as concerted music. Meanwhile the whole social organization of music had changed. Music made its way from the middle-class parlour to the gilded halls of the aristocracy. In the past there had been a general desire to make music, to take part in a concerted whole. From now onwards the virtuoso was to come to the fore and display his gifts. For reasons both of circumstance and of the nature of the art itself the chief embodiment of the new ideals was found among the composers of the Latin countries.

The form that the bass itself was to take now became a problem. In strictly monodic works it was originally completely subservient to the voice-part, which took its expression from the text; it was a mere harmonic foundation in long sustained notes. It remained so, in fact, in secco recitative as long as that tradition lasted. But more conservative composers — those of the Roman school, for example — treated the bass vocally and so preserved the original melodic character of the continuo. One of the best and simplest ways in which the contemporary feeling for form could be satisfied consisted in the repetition in the bass of a set theme — either long or short — over which the upper parts could develop freely without, however, sacrificing their dependence on the foundation. This device was known as the basso ostinato. Its use provided a reinforcement to music in the new concerted style and enabled it to form a properly balanced whole. By the end of the seventeenth century composers had succeeded in the invention of free basses which bore an artistically complete relation to the melodic concerted parts. Once again the bass gradually became a member with equal rights in a polyphonic body; and once it had acquired a melodic character, it had sounded its own death-knell. In Bach's "trios" — the violin and viola da gamba sonatas — the basso continuo was already forced to occupy an insignificant place; and in the chamber and orchestral music of the pre-Haydn period it disappeared for ever.

A particularly important part in the reformation of melodic structure was played by the vocal and instrumental art of the seventeenth century. The old vocal and instrumental embellishments were purely ornamental, the mere trappings of the essential melody; they were rarely expressive. In the new period, up to the end of the eighteenth century, the delight in improvised ornament was as active as ever, but a good deal of the ornamentation became stylized, without serious detriment to the basic melody. The best and most individual madrigal-composers, however — Marenzio, Monteverdi, and others — had already rescued their melodies from the caprice of singers (as Bach did later in a higher degree) and devoted their finest craftsmanship to providing their own embellishments; and in the same way the seventeenth century exerted itself to render its ornamentation expressive and to enlist melody and decorative invention under the same banner. The continued endeavour to achieve passionate utterance, sharp characterization, and vivid tone-painting played a vital part in originating the modern motif.

These were the factors that gave the new style of composition its general character in the seventeenth century. There was no fundamental difference between sacred concerted music, secular chamber music (the cantata and duet), opera, oratorio, or even instrumental chamber music. The ideal that inspired all these forms was song; and in this sense their development ran on identical lines. But the actual shapes they took were quite distinct. We may begin with the chamber cantata, since by its very nature it remained the most independent of external circumstances and, in addition to affording the purest example of the development of the seventeenth-century idea of form, provided composers with an experimental training-ground and the necessary equipment for opera and oratorio.

The cantata was a lyrical form in dramatic shape, a unique phenomenon akin to the modern ballad. Its particular manifestations showed no variety or individuality; as a form it was stereotyped and monotonous. Its natural emotion was not deep or heartfelt, but was expressed by superficial ornamentation. The pastoral, in its progress from the idyllic to the pathetic, remained its principal sphere, just as on the literary side it derived from the idylls of Theocritus and Virgil and Ovid's *Heroides*. The madrigal, both sacred and secular, had long before adopted a kind of narrative framework — later to be established as recitative — to which prominence was usually given by a homophonic treatment of the voices. Oddly enough, it was quite a long time before monody incorporated in the cantata the forms that had been at its disposal from the very first (the recitative-like madrigal and the air), or rather before it extracted from recitative the element of pure song and gradually made it independent. A characteristic of the cantata was the complete subordination of poetry to music, which quickly became established. In the sixteenth century the composer had regarded himself as the interpreter of the poet. Petrarch, Boccaccio, Sannazaro, and even Dante enjoyed a new popularity, thanks to the musicians; and Ariosto and Tasso were glorified in the settings of their verse. In monodic settings, too, the Florentines at least took poetry seriously. Caccini's musicianship was too weak to achieve anything more than conventional sentiment in the madrigal and modest grace in the song form. But a whole group of composers, with Monteverdi as their leader, aimed at truth and accuracy in the expression of emotion and did not shrink from employing any audacities of harmony or melody to attain their end.

The pursuit of this lofty ideal still required a definite poetic stimulus. But it was of short duration. Composers soon diverted their energies into a channel of sensuously beautiful melody, and for that they needed poetry that fitted most closely the musical forms they had won for their own. There arose an entirely new kind of *poesia per musica*, which lost in invention and content what it gained in flexibility and smoothness. This disjointed and unsound relationship between the sister arts at first gave the Italians the advantage, but later led to the impoverishment of their musical lyric and created that gap between folk-song and art-song which in German music was to be filled so wonderfully by the Lied. In Italy, however, this relationship was a practical necessity, since only on these lines was it possible to ensure normality in harmony and melody. In accordance, one might say, with the natural law of the conservation of energy, composers of cantatas and operas in the seventeenth century set aside conscious obedience to theoretical principles and devoted all their energies to writing music that obeyed its own laws.

The task that faced them was extraordinary and unprecedented. It was possible, of course, to borrow from folk-song and popular melody, and this was done to a greater or less degree. But on the whole the tendency was to move away from popular influences. The object was to establish quite independently the laws of pure monody from the structure of short themes to their combination in an elaborately articulated whole. The example of

Florence was followed by Rome, where men like MARIO SAVIONI, LUIGI ROSSI, MARC' ANTONIO CESTI and particularly GIACOMO CARISSIMI cultivated the cantata with passionate devotion and enlarged its possibilities of expression by giving greater scope to pathos, grace, and humour — the last a specialty of the Roman school. Nowhere does the cantata show such abundant variety of form as in the work of the Roman composers, such versatility in the combination of arioso and recitative, such natural ease and fluency of style. The rondo cantata, however, in which there was a lively treatment of a recurring arioso section, may be regarded as the favourite form. Contemporary with the Roman school of cantata-composers and succeeding them were the masters of Venice and northern Italy, led by Bologna. The cantata with instrumental accompaniment owed its typical form, after much tentative experiment, to ALESSANDRO STRADELLA of Modena; but the classical representative of the cantata's maturity in all its various forms and its most prolific composer was the Neapolitan ALESSANDRO SCARLATTI, who has left us in his cantatas an inexhaustible treasure of melodic invention and sensuous beauty. To him is due the definitive shape of the da-capo aria. In this form the claims of poetry are reduced to the most modest scale, so that music may as far as possible remain its own master and pursue its course unchecked. What the aria demanded of its text was simply the set form — principal section, middle section, repetition of principal section — a definite emotion, and nothing more unless it was a suggestion for a picturesque accompaniment, the object being to produce a kind of vocal sonata. In a later age, when naturalism was the vogue, it may have been regarded as a mistake that this vocal sonata should have been transplanted into opera; but the grandeur, richness, and fruitful possibilities of the form itself were demonstrated a hundred times over by Bach, Handel, Hasse, Jommelli, and Mozart.

The new style also took possession of the motet, which became the sacred cantata. If monody may be said to have brought emancipation to secular song, it threatened church music with a danger of which musicians of the time were fully aware. The evidence of that is the mass of church music in the old style, written by composers who were otherwise quite "modern"; and yet the right note was not truly struck. The sixteenth-century tradition survived most vigorously and most naturally at Rome, but Venetian composers like Antonio Lotti and Neapolitans like Alessandro Scarlatti also took a delight in conscious archaism. The age of innocence of a-cappella music, however, was over. The sacred cantata held the field and adapted itself readily enough, after a short florescence of monodic and concerted motets, to the forms of secular song, developing a tendency to abandon Biblical texts in favour of a fulsome religious poetry in the baroque manner. It was in the sacred cantata that the new relationship between vocal and instrumental parts developed and became firmly established. The concerted treatment of the parts in instrumental chamber music became the model for a similar treatment of vocal and instrumental parts in combination. In place of the merely ornamental contrasts of separate choirs to be found in earlier music, there prevailed from now on an ingenious and imaginative alternation of voices and instruments. The instrument anticipates the theme of the voice-part or develops it still further, and the parts interchange or combine with the utmost freedom and ease. Side by side with the creation of the small cantata came the establishment of the form on a large scale. The ornate Venetian church music became divided up into choruses and solo songs and readily embraced the new forms; the result was the " grand cantata," in which the claims of music involved the subjection even of the venerable text of the Mass itself. It was not in borrowed forms or in the use of instruments that the secularization of church music lay, but in the change of standpoint, the naked subjectivity, the all too personal relation of the worshipper to the Deity. In the music of the sixteenth century God's answer to prayer had been implicit in the supplication, but now the suppliant himself appeared upon the scene.

ACCOMPANIED MONODY

The development of opera ran on similar lines to that of the cantata, except that here the conflicting claims of drama and music naturally could never be completely reconciled. In individual cases drama continually succeeded in re-establishing its rights, but unfortunately this was generally done by a vaguely idealistic re-creation of Greek tragedy; the approach was literary and hence one-sided, and there was no proper consideration of the part that music had a right to play. How insignificant in effect the supposed realization of such ideals could be was shown by the first phase of the new form's development. For all that its earliest exponents did to bring it to life, Florentine opera would have remained a bloodless phantom, a merely temporary adjunct to the festivities of the Grand Duke's court, had not a composer of genius, CLAUDIO MONTEVERDI, at that time *maestro di cappella* to the Duke of Mantua, taken it in hand. The general structure of early opera was based on an entirely false conception, the engineer, the scene-painter, and the dancer being considered more important than the poet or the musician. In his *Orfeo*, produced at Mantua in 1607, Monteverdi showed for the first time that within this framework it was possible to create a living, passionate, intensely dramatic music. For the first time he allowed the instruments to speak a language of their own — though it is a mistake to assert that he already used them in the modern manner.

He won a place in the drama for instrumental music, which it was to lose all too soon; and if the use he made of it was concentrated, it was for that reason all the more brilliant.

Arianna (1608) seems to have made an even deeper impression than *Orfeo*. All that has survived is the famous Lament of the deserted heroine, which for many years was accepted as a model of its kind — music of immortal verity and loveliness. The operas that followed *Arianna* are completely lost, with the exception of two works of the great master's old age — he had since become *maestro di cappella* at St. Mark's, Venice (1613) — which reveal a ripe mastery of characterization, melody, and form. Through all Monteverdi's work runs the dramatic impulse; its quickening fire is felt in his a-cappella madrigals and imparts a glow to the masterpieces of subjective inspiration that he wrote for church and chamber. In his *Combattimento di Tancredi e Clorinda*, performed in 1624, he produced the first example of a genuine secular oratorio, though he was not actively concerned with the creation of a new form and indeed only considered the single detail of a new device of instrumentation worth mentioning. In his lifetime Monteverdi drew upon himself that hatred of the reactionaries which is the lot of genius. Even today no one can remain indifferent to the disturbing stimulus of his music. He is the greatest representative of a period of revolution in which the very foundations of tradition were shaken.

Florentine opera did not last long; and for that both circumstances and its own nature were responsible. It early won occasional acceptance in a number of Italian cities; but its first home that could in any sense be called permanent was in the cardinals' palaces in Rome. Here several important works were produced, in which the tendency was to abandon dramatic expression in favour of purely lyrical melody, under the powerful influence of the Roman cantata. Some of the opera librettos written by Giulio Rospigliosi, poet and later Pope, have a particular historical importance, since they provided for the first time a contrast to the sentimental pathos of the principal characters in the figures of low comedy, such as the page and the nurse. This mixture of styles was popular throughout the seventeenth century, until antiquarian purism stepped in and restored to opera seria its exclusively pathetic character.

A Roman was the author of these works, and it was mostly Roman singers who supplied the opera for the first permanent theatre at Venice (1637). For many years after that, Venice remained the principal home of opera in Italy, and, for that matter, in Europe. At first it set an example to other cities and produced its own operas; later, from the beginning of the eighteenth century, it continued, with its large number of public theatres, to act as a consumer. Venetian opera swung away more and more from the ideas of the first inventors of the form. FRANCESCO CAVALLI, a pupil of Monteverdi, was the most influential of the Venetian composers. He was a master of subtle characterization, who knew how to write recitative full of life and interest and succeeded in producing scenes that were genuinely dramatic and theatrically effective. But in the tender and appealing work of the Roman composer Marc' Antonio Cesti arioso was introduced into opera for its own sake. The solemn overture of Monteverdi and Cavalli was succeeded by the vivid, graphic, descriptive sinfonia of about 1660, to be followed in turn by the empty formality of the sinfonia of Venetian opera in its decline. The chorus of the Florentine operas became reduced to the insignificant interjections of supernumerary characters and often disappeared completely. Simple pastoral or mythological subjects were replaced by heroic or historical themes, in which the whole of ancient and early mediæval history was garbled to provide an excuse for love-intrigues. The librettist became the obsequious slave, first of the stage engineer and then of the composer, while the composer was more and more reduced to the role of an obliging purveyor of material for the castrato and the prima donna. Opera developed into a succession of arias, the business of simulating some dramatic connexion between them being relegated to recitative. A certain number of situations became stereotyped — scenes of eavesdropping, mistakes of identity, outbursts of jealousy, dreams and conjurations — and these continually offered a challenge to the skill of rival composers. The librettist's technique consisted in involving half a dozen pairs of lovers, with the addition of an odd supernumerary, in all sorts of entanglements and complications and then reconciling them all at the end. Thus opera, considered as an artistic whole, degenerated gradually into an æsthetic monstrosity, and as time went on, the objections to which it laid itself open grew stronger. But, for all that, its composers achieved wonders, not merely from the musical but also from the dramatic point of view. To appreciate the achievement of baroque opera we must take the framework of its style for granted, admitting as inevitable in the circumstances the large part played by convention.

This proviso is particularly necessary in the case of the Neapolitan school, which with its founder, Francesco Provenzale, and especially with its leader, Alessandro Scarlatti (1659–1726), was to break the Venetian influence. Scarlatti's dramatic talent was slight, but he was a great composer with an inexhaustible fount of melody, and he was responsible for finally establishing the form of the operatic aria, to which he contributed an increasing refinement of ornamentation and elaborate instrumental accompaniment. He marks the point of departure for the development of opera in the eighteenth century.

Opera as represented by the style of the Venetian school enjoyed a triumphal progress throughout Europe. France and Germany pursued different paths, in accordance with their different political circumstances. In France Italian opera was at first imported without great attempt at adaptation or reconstruction. Cardinal Mazarin invited an Italian opera company to perform in Paris in 1645. This incursion was followed by others; and in the 1660's Paris made the acquaintance of two important works by Francesco Cavalli. Meanwhile, however, the poet Perrin and the composer Cambert, cunningly using the ballet de cour as a basis, had attempted to create a truly national opera; their *Pomone* (1671) was performed at the opening of the newly founded " Académie de Musique," which, significantly enough, had been preceded about ten years before by a royal " Académie de Danse." Circumstances were against Perrin and Cambert, and their enterprise failed. A successor arose who took over their work with better fortune. This was GIAMBATTISTA LULLI, a Florentine, who basked in the gracious favour of the " Roi Soleil," and created the French heroic opera, with its two guiding stars —Love and Glory. In the form that he originated, with its magnificent array of dances and choruses, its characteristic and more richly accompanied recitative, the concise melodic style of its ariosi, and — most important of all — its continued, if only partial, adherence to a certain principle of dramatic propriety, it remained until the time of Gluck the shield and buckler of tradition and the repository of a jealously guarded style.

In England, too, opera began to take root in the court masques, a survival and an imitation of the festival performances that were all the rage in Renaissance Italy, in which originally music had only the modest task of supplying choral songs and accompaniments to the dances. The interpolation in Shakspere's *Tempest* is a typical masque of the period. From these masques there developed in the course of the seventeenth century a number of hybrid productions akin to opera, among them a work that, allegedly, was sung throughout — *The Siege of Rhodes* (1656), the text of which was by Sir William Davenant. It is difficult to say how it came about that England, where the door was always open to Italian influences, never created a national opera, as did Italy herself, France, and eventually Germany. The reason may be not so much a matter of history as of psychology and climate; it is to be found, perhaps, in the difference between the Italian and the English attitude towards music. Music is not the natural means of expression for the Englishman to the same extent as it is for the Italian. He regards it as something higher than a mere vehicle of the emotions and passions; and this explains why in England music remained in a subordinate position to drama. England produced instrumental pieces and ballets and created " supernatural " and " romantic " scenes; but, on the whole, English opera remained a " Singspiel," a spoken play with an abundance of complementary music. The actual musical life of England was to be found in the music that amateurs made for themselves in the home. Here the "fancy" was cultivated long after the rest of Europe had adopted the Italian concerted style and the virtuoso trio and solo sonata. The fancy, a polyphonic form written for the viol consort, had an intimate charm and attraction comparable only with that of the chamber music of the eighteenth century. HENRY PURCELL (1659–95), who wrote music for the theatre as well as an actual opera, was the last important creative force of a country which, as far as music is concerned, has since depended on foreign importations. Purcell may be compared to some extent with Mozart, not only on account of his tragically short career, but also because of the ease with which he assimilated foreign styles. He wrote trio sonatas in the Italian style; but in the strength of their melodic line they are still typically English, and so are his fancies, with their daring harmonic progressions. Beside his effective church music, which culminates in his magnificent *Te Deum*, his miniature opera *Dido and Æneas* stands on a pinnacle by itself, a model of pure and profound expression achieved by the most modest means.

In Germany the first growth of a national opera was nipped in the bud. HEINRICH SCHÜTZ wrote for the Saxon court in 1627 the first opera in German, *Dafne*, which was undoubtedly in the spirit of Monteverdi. Later a number of German courts tried the experiment of opera in the vernacular, not so much in South Germany and Austria, where Munich and Vienna both remained faithful to Italian opera, as in the centre and the north — at Brunswick, Hanover, and Weissenfels. At Brunswick there were two periods when German opera flourished, the second associated with a distinguished name, GEORG KASPAR SCHÜRMANN. Dresden soon deserted to Italian opera and remained faithful to it longer than any other German city. The glories of Leipzig, Nuremberg, and Augsburg pale beside those of Hamburg, where for fifty years an operatic tradition was kept alive which throws a melancholy light on the state of affairs in Germany at the time. There was a vague idea prevalent that it was the function of opera to be ennobling; and hence when the Hamburg opera was founded, in 1678, its secondary object was to provide edification and the first works produced were on Biblical subjects. Soon there was a serious decline. The operas became extremely crude and lost all consistency of style. German and Italian texts were combined without scruple or hesitation,

THE RENAISSANCE

and all sense of artistic and moral responsibility disappeared. Both by the choice of language and by the spirit in which the librettists approached their task German opera was doomed to failure. A producer of genius like the talented and enterprising JOHANN SIGISMUND KUSSER could lend the tottering structure for a short time the semblance of solidity; and a master of melody and colour like REINHARD KEISER was able to support it for several years. But in the end it was submerged and overwhelmed by the tide of foreign affectation. We shall see later how modest were the origins of truly national German opera, when at last the time was ripe for it.

For much the same reasons German song also deteriorated. The monodic movement from Italy might have led to a new growth of lyrical art if German poetry had been ready for it; but by the time it was able to provide musicians with the texts they wanted for the madrigal and the cantata the opportunity had passed. In the meantime the Thuringian composer HEINRICH ALBERT made tentative efforts to find suitable melodies for the strophic verses of the Königsberg poets; and what he aimed at and seldom achieved was brought to fulfilment by a master of song, ADAM KRIEGER. In these songs, which were adopted by students all over Germany, a wide range of emotions — from exuberant heartiness to youthful melancholy — found genuine and authentic expression. In the time of Albert and

Krieger and later, a whole mass of utterly inferior ditties also became popular throughout the country. Their vogue did not, however, prevent musicians from feeling a pronounced contempt for strophic song — the basis of the Lied; indeed, it makes such an attitude comprehensible. German song declined still further at the end of the century with the growing tendency to adapt words to existing dance-tunes and instrumental melodies, generally of fashionable French origin. The aria and the cantata choked the growth of the Lied. Only German sacred song, which found in PAUL GERHARDT a true poet, was still the inspiration of genuinely musical talent.

Instrumental Music in the Seventeenth Century

In instrumental music monody achieved an even more decisive victory of new over old than in vocal music. The disintegration that followed its introduction was more severe and the new edifice that it erected more striking. The culminating-point, to which the development of the sixteenth century had led up, was Giovanni Gabrieli's orchestral sonata, the basis of which was a concerted antiphony of contrasted masses of tone — such as strings and brass — and the contrast between sections consisting of contrapuntal imitation for the finer-toned instruments and homophonic movements built up on mighty pillars of sound, in which dance-rhythms were often employed and a strongly accented triple time was favoured. This use of sonorous tutti in the manner of a ritornello was adopted by Gabrieli from the canzon francese. A number of Venetian and north Italian composers cultivated this type of orchestral canzon for a short time, but it soon lost its independent existence as an instrumental form and dwindled to the short introduction to the grand cantata. Its grave and solemn movement and its use of the wind ensemble had a particular attraction for the German composers of church music and cantatas.

In Italy, however, it took on a new lease of life before it was finally submerged. The contrasted upper parts of the two concerted groups — a violin and a cornet, for example — were embroidered in the most elaborate fashion with ornaments, runs, trills, and arpeggios. The virtuoso advanced his claim, and an individual, subjective character began to appear in music for festivals and state occasions. In this way there came into existence quite early, as if by accident, the primitive form of the concerto grosso, in which, between the unvarying repetitions of a ritornello for the tutti, individual instruments indulged in virtuosity to their hearts' content. This form, the combination of so-called " symphonies " with solo improvisations, was undoubtedly much cultivated in Venice and Rome. Its weakness was that in spite of all its simplicity it lacked unity, the unity that could be achieved only by thematic association and coherence of ideas. No wonder, then, that the Venetian orchestral sinfonia disappeared completely and carried on, so to speak, an underground existence until it finally came to light again at the end of the seventeenth century at Rome, Bologna, and Modena — cities that boasted particularly flourishing musical academies. By this time it was able to take advantage of the new clarification of harmonic relationships and the extraordinary progress in the conception of writing for instruments that had been made in chamber music. The concerto grosso had appeared.

This development had begun with the canzon francese and continued in an uninterrupted straight line to the creation of modern sonata form, the last and most mature form of pure instrumental music. The canzon francese already contained the undeveloped germs of what was to come; in it the contrasts of time, tempo, and texture which were essential for an organically constructed instrumental composition were already foreshadowed. The appearance of the basso continuo helped to sharpen these contrasts. At first, until about 1620, the canzon regarded the continuo with suspicion, anxious as it was to avoid being compelled to surrender its essentially polyphonic character. Already, however, at this stage the component parts of the work became detached and took the form of separate, contrasted movements. The result was a chequered pattern, made up of short fughetta-like sections, dance-rhythms, and homophonic movements characterized by gentle melancholy or boisterous energy. " Capriccio " is the proper name for this transitional form, which continued for a long time to influence the composition of solo chamber music and concerted works for a few instruments. It was in this shape that the canzon was taken over by FRESCOBALDI. He was not, however, content with it as it stood; he felt a need for binding together at least the principal movements of this complex whole by means of thematic unity. In his works the theme of the first movement undergoes ingenious transformations, which are quite often barely recognizable, with different time-signatures and increasingly rapid tempos; while between the principal movements come free fantasias, serving as connecting links. Frescobaldi's use of this principle of variation, which runs through the whole of the instrumental music of the seventeenth century, had a particular influence on the German sonata-composers. To the neutral character of his thematic material, which did not appeal to the newly awakening taste for virtuosity, we must attribute the fact that his immediate influence made itself felt more strongly in compositions for clavier and organ than in chamber music. Also the type of canzon that aimed at developing the latent possibilities of a single theme and led eventually to Bach's fugue was soon relegated entirely to clavier music; it was incompatible with the art of the continuo.

At the same time the sonata for a few instruments with continuo never entirely gave up imitative treatment, and its principal movement always implied a grateful acknowledgment of its direct descent from the canzon francese. It had, in fact, taken over the lively imitations of the canzon and adapted them to new conditions. Not, of course, that the old polyphony in four, five, or even six parts disappeared completely even in the Italian continuo sonata of the seventeenth century. The natural result of a greater number of parts was a return to concerted music with contrasted groups of instruments, which paved the way for the concerto grosso. However, the principal effect the continuo had was to reduce the number of instrumental parts in the canzon. The small vocal concerto provided the model for the instrumental duet, which very soon secured general acceptance; it was usually written for two violins with continuo accompaniment, the bass being reinforced by another string instrument, the viola da gamba or the violoncello. In this trio sonata of the seventeenth century the strings gradually ousted the wind. All this sonata literature is eminently violin music, and it displays a very specific invention, which as time goes on grows more intense and purer, inspired by the particular charm of the instrument. The contrasts of legato and spiccato are in themselves almost a sufficient guide to the structural divisions of the sonata. The string family became the normal instrumental body, and in the relation between strings and wind we have the first sign of their arrangement in the modern orchestra.

In addition to these forms, which had their origin in the canzon, the sonata also adopted new ones whose principles were dictated by the continuo: improvisation and variation. The continuo gave free rein to virtuosity. Over long-sustained, slowly moving notes in the bass the sequence held high festival, sometimes to the point of riotous excess, content at first with empty formulas, but gradually developing a more supple type of figuration. Over a constantly repeated figure in the bass — the ostinato — composers erected an elaborate edifice of variations, designed to afford opportunities for a progressive show of virtuosity, the favourite culmination being a transformation to rapid triple time. Such methods soon made it possible to blend the set of variations with the variations-suite. The bass themes of variations of this kind, which were originally songs or dance-tunes, were reduced to pregnant harmonic formulas, thus forcing the concerted parts to be more concise and laying on them a heavier artistic

responsibility. At the end of the century the favourite type of variation form was the chaconne,
founded on a bass theme in triple time and fixed
rhythm.

From these various materials the early classical
sonata was built up. The time of uncertainty and
experiment passed extraordinarily quickly, and it
was not long before the development of the individual movements was achieved and a clear conception formed of the appropriate outlines of the
whole. Economy of means made it necessary to take
great pains in constructing the subjects of fugal
movements and the melodies of slow movements.
One of the most striking things in the history of
instrumental music is the way in which the blending of what may be called "neutral" themes and
brilliant figuration gave birth to the flexible modern
fugue-subject, with its strongly characteristic pro-
file, and, inspired by the elegiac arioso of the Roman and Venetian cantata, the instrumental "cantabile" appeared. In the movements that were
treated contrapuntally the idea of imitation had, so
to speak, to be discovered anew. The trio sonata
continued to cling to these movements, as a counter-
balance to the more superficial sections given up to
virtuosity. In them it found a reassurance against the
menace of dilettantism. In these "canzoni" (as the
more pretentious imitative movements of the sonata
continued to be called for quite a long time) atten-

tion was always paid to craftsmanship. As in the later chamber duet, it was regarded as a point of honour to write in canon; the trio sonata rarely descended to facile successions of thirds.

From the restless capriccio grew the " sonata da chiesa " or church sonata, which in its simplest form was based on a few simple contrasts expressed in the form of two pairs of movements. Each pair consisted of a slow and a quick movement; but to these were added contrasts of time and structure between the quick movements — one being in a more severe, the other in a freer, style — and of key between the slow movements. The decrease in the number of movements was accompanied by an increase in their scope and intrinsic value, by a greater consistency of emotional content between different movements and a more logical conception of the work as a whole. The principle of the capriccio, one is tempted to suspect, is to be found in a secret tendency towards program music. The church sonata, on the other hand, became in its purest form the most absolute music imaginable — if indeed there is such a thing as absolute music. It recalls the heroic atmosphere and elegiac mood of Poussin's landscapes. Fond though it is of chromatic themes, it restrains and sublimates all strong emotion. In the noblest melody, in the purest euphony, it found for the first time the laws of a cogent system of modulation. The language that it speaks with such restraint is not ours; yet this wealth of splendid music can still grip our attention, can even charm us and lay us under an enduring spell. For a whole century — from 1650 to 1750 — as long as the continuo maintained its vitality, the sway of the " sonata da chiesa " prevailed. The great names of its hey-day, which is associated with the churches and academies of Venice, Bologna, Modena, and Rome, were Legrenzi, Bassani, Vitali, and, above all, Corelli, dall' Abaco, and Handel; and Tartini and Gluck still paid it homage.

Beside the church sonata came the " sonata da camera " or chamber sonata, a succession of dance-movements with or without a freely constructed introductory movement. The idealized dance existed as early as the sixteenth century, and the oldest printed collections of dances for lute, keyboard instruments, or strings already show us not only individual movements of considerable melodic charm, often with variations, but also successions of typical dance forms, knit together by a less rigid principle of variation — in other words, the origins of the suite. In Italy the incentive offered by the dance was directed to the service of chamber music and the concerted and monodic styles, and, just as in Germany, the variations-suite was cultivated as well as the succession of independent dance-movements. The composition of the suite changed in accordance with the constant reaction of the dance itself to new

113

influences, principally French. About 1660, mainly through the example of the French lutenists and the clavier composers who followed in their footsteps, a stock succession of movements became established, in which the rhythmic life of the dance found its ideal expression. These were the sober allemande, the brisk courante, the slow and melancholy sarabande, and the lively gigue. Between the sarabande and the gigue it was usual later on to insert the little characteristic dances, which became fashionable through the French dancing-masters' insatiable passion for novelty — the minuet, passepied, rondeau, bourrée, gavotte, and the rest. In Italy, where the inclination towards chamber music was so strong, these dances became stylized, which made it easier for them to merge into the movements of the church sonata. The allemande would take the place of the canzon, and the sarabande that of the slow second movement. The intrusion of the lighter types of dance-movement led eventually to the church sonata's having to exchange its first home for the secular music-room. For that matter, the Church from the beginning of the eighteenth century demanded music more elaborately scored and more splendid in effect — the full panoply of the orchestra.

In Germany it was different. There the dance-movement and the suite were only united to the continuo after some difficulty. There was a reluc-

tance to give up polyphony, and the bright boisterous wind instruments were preferred to the aristocratic violin. The result was open-air rather than
chamber music. The same composers who extended
so enthusiastic a welcome to the Italian dance-song
produced in their dance-movements the healthiest,
the most popular, the most characteristically German music imaginable. The growing influence of
the South affected the stability of the German suite.
The gay pieces for wind instruments, intended for
performance in the open air, suffered least. Their
joyous irresponsibility is seen at its best in the en-
gaging " tower sonatas " (music to be played from
the towers of churches and other public buildings)
written at the end of the century by men like
Petzel and Reiche. Just when the German suite
stood at the parting of the ways between chamber
and orchestral music Lulli came to the rescue with
his ballet suite. The Germans reacted gladly to this
new stimulus.

The reason is not far to seek. The Lullian suite,
with its five-part writing which treated even the
lowest instruments as individuals, could be linked
up with the tradition of the old variations-suite.
Moreover, it was admirably suited to the new home
of the suite, the middle-class and student collegia
musica, whose members were anxious to have something for their fingers to do and thoroughly enjoyed
taking an active part in music that was full of sub-

stance and energy. At the same time Lulli's opera overture — the "French" overture, as it is called — became the normal introductory movement of the German suite, after successive attempts had been made to adopt the intrada, the canzone, and the Italian sinfonia in the form of the capriccio or the Venetian opera symphony. There was once more genuine orchestral music. In addition to the body of strings concerted parts were also written for wind instruments, either the two oboes and bassoon of Lulli's trios or — better still — two trumpets (clarini), which emphasized the popular character of this type of music-making. For nearly fifty years the "ouverture," as the ballet suite was christened after its introductory movement, was the favourite music of the German collegia. The best composers produced examples of the form, containing a rich store of healthy and joyous melody. Some, such as Kusser, Erlebach, Georg Muffat, and J. K. F. Fischer, attached themselves more closely to the French model and, like the minor French composers, continued to draw inspiration from the stage and dances of the day. Others, among them Bach and also Telemann, Fasch, and Förster, made the form a vehicle for music of wider range and greater depth. At the same time the new enthusiasm for orchestral music was an aid to the pure development of German chamber music. The organists and town musicians of North Germany, influenced partly by the Italians and partly by the English, took a particular interest in the trio sonata — with this difference, however, that instead of two violins they preferred to write for violin and bass viol (viola da gamba). Thanks to the bass viol, which was peculiarly the virtuoso instrument of the North, they indulged more than the Italians in variation and fantasy.

Instrumental monody — the solo sonata — had the hardest task. The sixteenth-century tradition that it had to build upon consisted principally of a riotous luxuriance of ornamentation. This had taken two forms — the coloratura treatment of a vocal melody and the variation of dance-tunes; but in neither case was there as yet any notion of organic principles of melody. The vehicle of the new instrumental monody was not at first a primarily melodic instrument, such as the violin or cornet, but one whose natural function was to play a bass part — the bass viol. For this there were very good reasons. With its large number of strings and aptitude for rapid movement, it was, like the lute, naturally suited to be the instrument of virtuosity. Already in the sixteenth century, in Spain, Italy, and particularly England, it was much used for improvisation, the favourite form being the varying of a short bass theme, possibly taken from a song- or dance-melody. It had also adopted from the lute the practice of playing chords and presenting the semblance of polyphony, and this enabled it to combine melody and accompaniment in the most ingenious and suggestive manner. In England the bass viol was still cultivated at a time when the violin was triumphing everywhere else, just as the elegant "fancy" remained popular after the rest of Europe had given a welcome to a more brilliant concerted style. CHRISTOPHER SIMPSON's *Division Violist* (1659) was the classic instruction-book for English players. It was more than a mere technical treatise; it was rather a dignified school of improvisation and of all the forms in which that art was exercised. The bass-viol style of playing formed the foundation of the violin sonata, which inherited from it the partiality for embroidering a bass with brilliant runs, arpeggios, and other embellishments. From the bass viol the violin also acquired its love of variation, as well as its readiness to abandon the continuo and build up a polyphonic structure out of its own resources. The tradition of this style was preserved for many years in the German violin sonata. We owe to it the marvels of Bach's unaccompanied sonatas and partitas.

In Italy, too, composers began by transferring the canzon and the fugue to a solo instrument and assigned an increasingly important place in the violin sonata to the movement that represented an extract from a polyphonic composition. Corelli in his epoch-making Op. 5 (1700) handed on to the eighteenth century the form of the fugue, in which the majority of the parts were entrusted to the solo instrument. TARTINI, too, in a great number of his sonatas helped the instrument in this way to attain its ascendancy. The best balance between the two partners in the solo sonata is probably to be found in the work of ANTONIO VERACINI and EVARISTO FELICE DALL' ABACO. These composers succeeded in dividing equally between the two parts the harmonic material of a fugal movement with one or two subjects. After dall' Abaco there appeared the solo sonata with clavier obbligato. The duties of the accompanist became more and more responsible and it was no longer safe to leave his share to the accidents of improvisation. The second half of the eighteenth century may in fact be said to have been the age of the clavier sonata with a more or less obbligato part for the violin. All that remained open to the violin as a solo instrument, apart from the concerto, was the study.

The solo sonata, in common with the trio sonata, made use of several forms; but the one that had a particular importance in its history was the first movement of the chamber sonata, which was in two sections. Its origin was the allemande, but as time went on, it showed less and less trace of its ancestry in a dance form. Contrasts in its melodic structure appeared quite early. An idea would be stated and answered, the contrast being generally between the flowing legato melody natural to the allemande and elaborate figuration in the virtuoso style. It was in this form that the new principles of instrumental cantabile were first established. In the first half of the eighteenth century there was a continual increase in the length of movements and in the emphasis laid on contrast; the widely accepted transformation of the style of the concerto to the solo sonata was a sign of the times. The spans and stresses of the rising edifice grew more ambitious, until finally the last vestiges of the old style were thrown aside; the moving bass and the restrictions of a definite metrical scheme lost their binding force. The early classical sonata discovered sonata form for its first movement; and with the discovery of the form came a new spirit — the "dramatic" spirit of modern music.

At the end of the seventeenth century the grand orchestral sonata also reappeared in a particular form which was rich in possibilities for the future — the concerto grosso and the solo concerto. The name "concerto grosso" was first applied to the orchestral sonata; but the term also included the church sonata and later the chamber sonata with massed strings, so that "concerto" in this case referred to the method of performance. But the name also described a particular formal structure; and from the first quarter of the seventeenth century it was used exclusively in this sense. In the concerto grosso a number of characteristic effects of contrast were brought to life and fitted together in a properly adjusted whole. The old delight in pitting different blocks of instrumental tone against one another was revived in the form of a strongly marked contrast between a ritornello for full orchestra and a concertino for solo instruments. In Italy the concertino was generally written for two violins and violoncello, but the Germans preferred various solo wind instruments. This contrast between the forte of the tutti and the fainter sound of the solo instruments gives us a clear idea of the simple conception of musical dynamics that prevailed at the time. There was a further contrast between the simple melodic character of the ritornello and the impetuous virtuosity of the solo sections.

In the trio sonata and the solo sonata of this period the contrast between plain melody and its elaborate transformation by virtuosity had not yet been perfectly adjusted; and this is true even of Corelli's famous Op. 5. In the concerto grosso this contrast found at last its legitimate home and its æsthetic justification. The statement of the theme by the full orchestra, then contention and rivalry, assent or contradiction, on the part of the solo instruments, interruption and prolongation, digression or return to the starting-point, subordination of the orchestra to the soloist or the group of soloists — all this gave the concerto's three movements such intense vitality, such a wealth of new associations, that it is not surprising that from Italy it quickly passed to Germany and England and carried all before it. Practically all the streams of instrumental composition in the seventeenth century flowed into the concerto grosso; but a special contribution was made by the Venetian opera overture with its trumpet solos and by Lulli's overtures and chaconnes, in which short compact episodes and variations were entrusted to a wood-wind trio. ARCANGELO CORELLI seems to have followed a different line of approach. The wealth of musical resources in Rome and a natural inclination to give his virtuosity wider scope may have led him consciously to combine the old ritornello symphony and the trio sonata. The immortal service that he rendered to music was the significant incorporation of the several parts in an essentially artistic whole.

The solo concerto appeared later than the concerto grosso. In the work of its first important exponent, the Bolognese composer GIUSEPPE TORELLI, the form is still primitive; the solo instrument is merely used to relieve the tutti and deals with the same material. As it developed, however, along the path that led to Tartini and Viotti, the combination of rival elements became more and more dramatic and the alternation of solo and tutti was dictated less by considerations of structure and tone than by an artistic impulse governing the whole.

The concerto grosso became the favourite instrumental form of the period. Composers, players, and listeners were all infatuated with it. Soon the resources it employed were multiplied, in accordance with the tendencies of the baroque period, and there was a return to the more massive structure of the old choral style. Alternatively the possibilities of tone-painting were exploited, as in the work of ANTONIO VIVALDI. The purest and noblest memorials of the Italian style are Handel's concerti grossi; of the German, with its greater variety and characteristic inflections, Bach's "Brandenburg" concertos, though their individuality and wealth of dynamics and expression take them far beyond the limits of the mere type. In the second half of the eighteenth century the concerto grosso declined, while the solo concerto continued to flourish. From the dissolution and decay of the older ideal the new symphonists took the materials with which, after a momentous period devoted to chamber music, they were to build their edifice.

Protestant Church Music

It is the glory of a few great and many lesser, devoted, humble Protestant masters that German music in the seventeenth century did not wholly merge into the stream of forms from Italy. Protestant sacred music had first of all to define its relation to the new instrumental style; here as in the Italian motherland the old persisted vigorously beside the new. It did so chiefly in the sumptuous Venetian motet forms, with their many voices and many choirs, whose most temperamental and colour-loving exponents were MICHAEL PRAETORIUS and JOHANN HERMANN SCHEIN. Praetorius revelled in the wealth of opportunity they afforded for vocal and instrumental settings, and sought to bind them with the chorale-melody in Florentine finery. The north Italian influences were developed with more independence, energy, and imagination by the St. Thomas cantor, Schein, in his choral motets, charged with overflowing strength, and his sacred concertos, with their richly contrasting patterns. Beside the large-scale motets with their demand, too, for an important body of instrumentalists, which had retained an extraordinary vitality, went the modest vocal motets for choirboy services — models at the same time for more rural use — in which the minor Thuringian cantors especially have handed down a treasury of simple yet full-sounding music, music homely and popular, yet reflective and filled with the genuine polyphonic spirit.

The master who sought to win a place in German

124

church music for the new monodic, concerted music originating in the South was HEINRICH SCHÜTZ (1585–1672), one of the greatest German composers. The chorale played an unimportant part in his work; he made it his mission to win for his nation and creed dramatic music in all its true forms. He was twice in Italy, first as a personal pupil of Giovanni Gabrieli, then as a spiritual disciple of Monteverdi. From 1617 till the end of his life he was active at the Dresden court chapel. After a decade happily spent in organization, he toiled to check the effects, so fatal to art, of the Thirty Years' War. Three times he attempted to escape by travelling to Denmark. At the end of his long life, tired out, he willingly handed over the reins to the Italians, who were becoming more and more favoured in Dresden. This man of deep inwardness of character and tender sensibility, destined to live in a stormy age and isolated in his career and in his work, is of all artists one of the most moving, most ideal figures. He was well aware of the danger of dilettantism inherent in monody and issued warnings against it verbally and in three great publications of different character, in which he pointed to the permanent worth of the pure a-cappella style, and thus helped to ensure that the German composers down to Bach should never, like the Italians, have to keep it artificially alive.

Otherwise he accepted the new forms both enthusiastically and deliberately and sought to mould them to the character of the German language and infuse them with German warmth. In accordance with his two visits to Italy, one part of these works has affinities with Gabrieli's music in the splendid drive of its vocal and instrumental style — in this way Schütz perfected for Germany the model of the great free church cantata — and the other the music of Monteverdi and Alessandro Grandi. Out of the spirit of monodic song, the sphere of small vocal and instrumental media and their combination with choir and orchestra, there grew a wealth of ingenious, expressive forms. There is in this music a sense of springlike awakening, a continuous stirring of dramatic life. From the motet grew the oratorio *scena;* and in late old age, after many other attempts in the oratorio style, Schütz wrote down his conception of the dramatic rendering of the Passion in three separate settings. Here, as always, his expression was of the keenest, not shrinking from the most daring resources of harmony and melody, yet always very simple and genuine. In his urge towards the utmost truth of expression, in his aversion to all surface polish for the sake of mere formal beauty, and at the same time in the instinctive sureness of his construction, Schütz, here where he is greatest, is comparable only to a great German painter — Albrecht Dürer.

Schütz's Faustian spirit was not inherited by any

of his imitators and pupils, not even by Andreas Hammerschmidt — by virtue of his suave, attractive melody the most influential among them — whose ingenious *Dialogues* were the favourite form of religious music. The variety and fluency of Schütz's forms suffered a limitation to a small number of fixed formal types, to a more traditional way of handling the relationship between voice and instruments. At the same time there were in comparison with the Italian cantata a few distinguishing features. The favourite voice of the Italians was the soprano, of the Germans the bass. Furthermore, in the German cantata the instrumental part is far more exuberant. There is no limit to the number of ritornellos and sinfonias.

But in one respect Schütz's contemporaries enormously enriched the church cantata, increasing its content both in form and in poetic expression by their use of the chorale. Through the chorale a piece of mediæval Netherland tradition, which might otherwise not have survived so long, was rescued for a later age. But the difference between the employment of the Gregorian and the Protestant chorale is nevertheless great. Through its compact, popular form, through its long exercise as congregational song, the Protestant chorale had attained a purer crystallization than the Gregorian had ever done. It had become not merely the liturgical but also the poetic kernel of church music. It was never to be used as a mere connecting link, to disappear from the artistic whole; whenever it emerges it does so as a living organism, always drawing attention to itself as a symbol of the universal and the divine. That this came to pass is to the credit of the German organists who understood Samuel Scheidt's decisive achievement and did not let it pass unheeded.

The organ assumed an ever greater importance in public worship. A second work of SCHEIDT, dating from 1650, testifies to one of its functions, that of accompanying congregational singing with the melody unaltered, while giving prominence and life to the subsidiary voices — a challenge to the profoundest harmonic interpretation, which no one before Bach was able fully to meet. Another of the organ's functions was to play the Magnificat responses, in which the dependence on liturgical motives and respect for the church modes — originally insisted upon — diminished more and more, so that eventually they were developed into a kind of school of fugue, with completely free thematic treatment. A third function was the elaboration of the chorale during Communion and the playing of preludes and postludes when hymns were sung by the congregation. In the course of all this the chorale was treated in every conceivable way. Variations could be made upon it, perhaps for home use on the clavier; the theme of the first line could be worked fugally, or the melody ornamented and introduced over a ground bass; or — and this was the ideal way — the simple melody could be both contrasted with and related poetically to the contrapuntal imitation of the subsidiary voices.

Most influential in this connexion was the work of Johann Pachelbel of Nuremberg, whose education and widespread activities made him — like Gabrieli and Sweelinck previously — one of the most important disseminators. He was the chief representative of the South German style of organ-playing, with its highly varied treatment of the chorale and close connexion with the liturgy. The North German masters, with Vincent Lübeck and Dietrich Buxtehude at their head, turned rather to freer forms. They expanded the toccata, the fantasia, the capriccio, and the ricercar and filled them with imaginative content, while their attitude towards the chorale was more subjective and, one might almost say, less respectful.

What was suitable to the chorale on the organ was suitable also in vocal music. It was introduced into the new free concerted motets as a symbol of the divine — as comfort, admonition, and promise — and in contrast to the human. The text had become in the course of time so intimately bound up with the melody that the chorale played by instruments alone could find a still more subtle and artistic employment and express a still profounder meaning. An old, yet new, polyphonic music, suggestive of the early motets, came to light again; only what had once been meaningless combination was now instinct with poetry. This poetical treatment of the chorale was applied to all the new examples of concerted motets which arrived from Italy with every fresh generation of composers. It remained also when, about 1700, some of the German church-cantata librettists, who had hitherto contented themselves with chorale and Biblical texts, or at the most with strophic songs on a small scale, introduced the great, free lyrical forms of the Italians — the recitative and the aria. Whereas Schütz had already stood for an exclusively musical approach, there now arose sacred music of the most subjective kind; and it was only natural that, especially in pietistic circles, sharp opposition should have been aroused by this operatic treatment of the divine service. In point of fact, Bach alone succeeded in so sublimating the baroque spirit of this style of church music that down to this day even the most susceptible have hardly been able to object to the use of contemporary secular sources in his art.

Bach

What is there not to be found in the Bach cantata, sacred or secular! There are the grand Italian aria for one or more voices, accompanied by a simple continuo or by several instruments, the arioso, the recitative. There are choral motets, homophonic or fugal, there are concerted choral movements with the richest alternations of chorus and soli. The treatment of the chorale-melody exhausts possibility, from the plainest four-part harmonization upwards. In the introductions the orchestral symphony is represented from its earliest Gabrielian shape to the contemporary French overture, and on to the modern concerto form. All these things the greatest of musicians welded in that spiritual and melodic furnace which was Bach's and Bach's alone, into such a unity that the problems of style presented by his tentative predecessors in their essays to balance vocal and instrumental elements sink into nothingness.

Bach was a great river into which all things flowed; and all that his own age and the ages before him had done and dreamed of were his tributaries. That old polyphonic language that was his was in his generation not commonly to be found in this strength and naturalness; it was the outburst of waters from long-hidden springs. Symbolic is Bach's origin in the heart of Germany, sprung of a family of organists and town-bandsmen, then the most musical section of German society. In a family circle of relations by blood and relations by art, near and far, he found the first sustenance for a mind greedy for learning. He began in the field of clavier music and of the motet and cantata. He went on to the organ school of Pachelbel and Buxtehude. Nothing that France or Italy could provide in the way of stimulus but was eagerly apprehended; not a stone was rejected, but every available one was put to an apt purpose in the building of his art. He delighted in kindling his imagination at alien fires; themes from foreign lands attracted him. He would take up whole compositions by other composers and with his own more vigorous breath inspire them with new life. His passacaglia would not have existed without Buxtehude; nor the *"Forty-Eight"* (*Das wohltemperirte Clavier*), had it not been for an opuscule, *Ariadne Musica* (1715), by a gifted harpsichordist, J. K. F. Fischer; nor his harpsichord suites without the preparatory work done in that vast field by the French. But he could touch nothing that did not grow under his hand to the utmost completeness and grandeur. All things flourish with him like the trees of the forest, broad-crowned and superb, and inevitable alike in the grandest branching polyphony and the most delicate of melodic sprays and blossoms. His polyphonic habit of thought led him along harmonic ways that, while not unlawful, were yet of the utmost daring. He was the first to make free and assured use of the possibilities of equal temperament (the division of the octave into twelve equal semitones, which had been effected finally and definitely by his contemporary Andreas Werckmeister), by completing the cycle of keys.

The art of the Bach cantata is an exposition of the foundations and principles of the Christian faith, and none more searching or more inexorable, deeper or more precise has ever been. The temporal life and the eternal, works and faith, mortality and death, sin and repentance, suffering and salvation — all the emotions and inspirations of the Christian soul exalted this, the greatest of preachers since Luther, not to theological abstractions, but to a passionate presentation by symbolic means of an incomparably vivid musical imagination. Bach's cantatas are truly a musical *biblia pauperum*. Joyous he could be, no man more so, as countless pages of his instrumental music show; but in the depths of his nature he was preoccupied with the mystery of man's end and the soul's yearning for redemption. A mystical rapture seizes him at the thought of the body's doom and the soul's hereafter.

Only in recent times has the world begun to apprehend Bach's unique musical imagination aright.

So searching was his vision that his themes tell us unmistakably the conception he formed of the attributes of God the Father, of Christ as Lord, Redeemer, and Victor, of the Devil as tempter, serpent, and adversary. It is not that his imagination is a storehouse of ready-made motifs; rather is it the universe of a supreme creative power, crowded with the vital forms of his begetting. And it is not that his musical symbolism is primarily dependent upon the text. While the themes of his choral fugues and motets are marvels of concentrated eloquence and spirit, mysteriously inexhaustible, his recitative (which has practically nothing in common with the Italian secco) incomparably unites a free and precise verbal expression with rhythmic decision, a wealth of music and formal strength. It is a whole, not a complement. As for the Bach aria, it is a monumental entity, yet filled with passionate thought and capable of the utmost flexibility.

And he, the most subjective and personal of polyphonic composers, felt more strongly than any other of his cantata-writing contemporaries the right of the chorale to the central place in his work. Hardly one of the two hundred cantatas that have come down to us is without its chorale; if in no other form, at least as a simple conclusion, with wonderfully expressive harmonies, to give as it were in the most concentrated form an ideal representation of the community. The symbolic outline of the hymn appears in movements of apparently the freest construction. Bach's favourite form in his choral cantatas (about a quarter of the whole were solo cantatas) is a kind of adaptation of the chorale prelude, in which the objective hymn, sung in the treble, is set off by the more subjective utterances of the lower voices and the orchestral commentary. The rhetorical effects obtained by a show of increasing animation play no part in the Bach cantatas. Here the mere statement of the hymn, following upon a brilliant movement, declares by its very plainness the depth of its significance. Intensity, in those of Bach's greater works that were conceived as a whole, is achieved by the sheer weight of the matter of the music and its inevitable development. Nowhere, it may be said, is Bach the man seen to be more radically possessed than in these works: the festal *Magnificat* and the two surviving examples of his Good Friday music which treat of the Passion and Death of Jesus — the *Passion according to St. Matthew*, a communal drama of a compassion all-comprehending and an intuition unapproachable, and the *Passion according to St. John*, an absorbed contemplation of the mystery of the divine person of Christ. Finally, in the *Mass in B minor* Bach miraculously realized all that was most complete, comprehensive, and objective in his conception of the essence and being of Christianity. Supreme musicianship, the utmost vividness of imagination, and the profoundest capacity for emotion were in Bach made one.

His instrumental music ranges over a perhaps still wider spiritual field. Also in this field he epitomizes the centuries and the nations. It is as though the seventeenth-century Italians had only striven to develop all instrumental forms while leaving perfection for him; it is as though François Couperin, the great master of the harpsichord, and himself the completion of the work of three generations, had developed the French clavier suite to a high point only in order to give Bach a stimulus. Part of this side of his work, too, was dedicated to the Church. Those eminently programmatic compositions, the chorale preludes, in whose narrow room life lives at its utmost intensity, give us the range of his feeling, as likewise does the superb architecture of the organ preludes and fugues, which are also program music, generally devotional in content. But who shall tell the wealth of this man's mind, revealed in the sparkling life of the orchestral suites, in the concertos, in the intimate utterances of his chamber sonatas, in the countless works of every sort with which he endowed the domestic keyboard instruments — toccatas, preludes, fugues, variations, partitas, and suites! Every instrument that was capable of polyphonic expression received his outpourings. To the harpsichord he makes a present of the Reincken chamber sonata, the " Italian concerto," the new solo sonata. The violoncello is set to play suites; proud fugues and the mighty *Chaconne* are entrusted to four fiddlestrings. He experiments; he makes a mixture of all kinds of forms — and out of it emerges as a matter of course a perfect shape. Bach's fugue is the consummation of the species. His theme is always an unmistakable individual in a definite situation, a creature born to experience; and its experiences correspond to its character. Hence no two fugues are alike in form, though all are consummate in their various ways. If that art whose spiritual content is the most concentrated has the best prospect of a long life, then will the inventions and sinfonias, and the preludes and fugues of the "*Forty-Eight*" endure for ever. The works of the last phase, the *Musical Offering* and *The Art of Fugue*, belong to what Goethe called "the supreme works of art which are frankly unprepossessing; they are ideals, which can and should be only approximately pleasing — æsthetic imperatives." Bach is of the company of those masters with whom every age and every individual must arrive at a new understanding; and still his greatness has not been appraised, nor can be ever.

Handel

Handel's greatness rests on quite other foundations than Bach's. The childish observation has been made that Handel wrote a heap of indifferent works which Bach had too thorough a training and too simple an eye to pure music to do; and this has brought upon him the misunderstanding of sciolists and even of masters. But Bach himself, Mozart, and Beethoven thought otherwise; and indeed Handel, if we take his personality as a whole, stands as little below Bach as Bach is below him. He was one of those musicians who only late in life discover and embrace their true vocation. Like Bach he ripened early; but while Bach undertook those journeys — the farthest of them to Hamburg — in which he learned his art, only in order to enrich his mind and then to retreat again into himself, Handel felt impelled, both as a musician and as a man, to grow continually in breadth and freedom. Hamburg first, then Italy — opening out to his sturdy, healthy German musicianship as the school of pure, true, classical melody — and finally England; these are fixed as the stations in the upward climb of a heroic life. And his exceptional productivity, in instru-

138

mental works, in church music in the grand manner, and in opera — he wrote about thirty Italian operas for London — was the preparatory school for his own particular creation, oratorio.

Oratorio had, when it came into Handel's powerful grasp, already had a long and interesting history. As originally conceived, it was the means which the Roman Counter-Reformation had specifically adopted to combat the seductive lure of secular art and to defeat it with its own weapons, by employing it in the church for devotional purposes. It might use Italian words or the rather more solemn tone of Latin, but in either case it took over all the forms of secular art that were current in the sixteenth and seventeenth centuries — in historical order, frottola, villanella, canzonetta, madrigal, and solo cantata or choral cantata, large or small. Its subjects, inherited from the age-old mystery plays, were the stories and episodes of the Old and New Testament and the legends of the saints. These it set in a framework of two parts comprising the edifying message, and connected them at first by narrative, but afterwards gave them dramatic form. In Carissimi's hands it had burgeoned as a Latin choral work, but by Handel's time it had blossomed into Italian oratorio, and as such had become a substitute during Lent for the opera and its solo work. The characteristics that distinguished the oratorio style from the operatic lay in the appeal to the hearer's imagination, in the incentive to, and the justification for, a more delicate moulding of the musical material, and especially in the more extended use of the chorus.

The way in which Handel met the claims of oratorio is to be explained, not historically, but only by the native sway of his whole mood and musical personality. About half of his oratorios, eighteen of them perhaps, are dramas of imagination. Taking the Jewish nation as his instance, he follows the fortunes of a chosen people, he depicts their champions and their adversaries; and he does this with a greatness and simplicity, with a variety of detail and a pictorial grasp, at times, too, with a sense of humour, that argue alike the great musician, the great dramatist, and the great man. The Florentine dream of the renascence of classical drama here comes true. A Greek would probably at once have understood the position and the meaning of the chorus in Handel's oratorio. The two oratorios which have done most to establish his fame, *Israel in Egypt* and *Messiah*, stand apart. *Israel*, that mighty choral oratorio, shows how a people of God lives and grows in history. *Messiah* dispenses entirely with action and resolves every event into emotion, and in that way shows how the promises of Christianity are fulfilled. The two together constitute a free confession of religious faith comparable only to that of Bach's B minor Mass, which had been completed but a short time before.

HANDEL

Great as is the sheer musical power that is shown everywhere in these works, especially in the choruses, which achieve the mightiest effects with the simplest means, it is not there that we look for the full import of Handel's creations. There can be no greater mistake than to fancy that the oratorio was nourished on ecclesiastical ground. On the contrary, it ranks with the opera as a free artistic effort, for in it for the first time a great artistic personality is speaking to his ideal public, to a nation and not to a parish. Handel's achievement is the preparation for what Beethoven afterwards did with the symphony; and it is on this eminence that these two masters, so utterly unlike, meet as conquerors. The performances of Handel's oratorios, particularly of *Messiah*, first in the British Isles and then in Germany, invigorated the whole of musical public life; they enfranchised art and addressed it to the world at large instead of to the narrow circle of connoisseurs.

MODERN TIMES

Homophony

BACH and Handel, composers of true polyphonic mettle, project, in their latest works, into a period that had long followed other ideals. The age of the figured bass ends in the triumph of homophony. As early as 1737 a champion of the moderns, Johann Adolph Scheibe, had stigmatized Bach's music as turgid and confused; and Jean-Jacques Rousseau gave even more one-sided expression to the spirit of the times when he advocated the cult of melody

142

and turned his back on any harmonic solidity and still more on any counterpoint. Great was the decline from the native strength of the overtures of composers such as Bach and Fasch to the symphonic output of Italians or Italianate Germans, from the sonatas of Corelli or Abaco to those of Nardini or Pugnani with their feminine endings, their repetitions that protracted without enhancing, their windy effeminacy, their impotence in expression, and their substitution of noise for vigour. The change of taste can be read in their basses. These had once been part of the thematic structure, but now they move inconsequently in support of the harmonies with unwilling feet, at the most enlivened by subdivision into idle semiquavers. With that, all melodic expression evaporated in endless *fioriture*.

We are now in the classical age of instrumental and vocal virtuosity, for which, however necessary as a brilliant school of melody, the historians have hardly had a good word. They found their scapegoat in Neapolitan opera as it developed after the death of Alessandro Scarlatti. Neapolitan opera had, indeed, abandoned itself with so little reflection to the lure of purely sensuous melody and done such violence to any kind of dramatic truth that the real motive for change came from within. JOHANN ADOLPH HASSE, the man of the moment, who set the librettos of Zeno and Metastasio to the entire satisfaction of Italy and Germany, had now reached the limit of what could be achieved by that tenderness and grace that came to him by nature. His greatest successor in the operatic field, NICCOLO JOMMELLI, who followed him in European favour, refined his orchestral accompaniment by an extended range of expression. In its *accompagnato* the orchestra seized upon the moments of passionate crisis in the recitative before the aria begins, and therein taught itself a hitherto unsuspected versatility, while the aria itself enlarged its repertory of forms. From the early years of the eighteenth century æsthetic theory took a lively interest in all operatic problems. Debate grew heated on the relative merits of the two national operas, Italian and French; recourse was had to classical drama in order to reach a genuine and independent conception of what opera should be. French opera showed itself impervious to any influences from the South, and attained, under its greatest master, RAMEAU, alone, within the limits of its traditional style, a refined and stable culture; whereas an Italian, TRAETTA, sought to unite the beauties of both operas.

The real reform of opera came from CHRISTOF WILLIBALD GLUCK, a master who, like Archimedes with his spiral, found his point of leverage outside what could strictly be called music and whom his enemies accordingly accused of making music without music. For this he called to his aid a man of fine intellect, whose instincts were æsthetic rather than poetical: Ranieri da Calzabigi. Gluck's actual achievement was the building and shaping of a new form of opera, and there was no way of doing this without a violent attack by every weapon of literary polemics upon the prevailing tradition. Fundamentally the attack was directed not so much against the arbitrary caprice of singers, with all its destructive effect on the sense of the drama, nor even against the convention of the male soprano. It is true that Gluck dispenses with coloratura, but he makes the severest demands of the Italian school on his singers; Orpheus is, after all, essentially a castrato role. The attack was aimed rather at the opera libretto of his time, which had reached its most beguiling literary form in Metastasio's much lauded dramas, set to music hundreds of times — and even by the young Gluck himself. The opera of intrigue, clad in historical or classical garb, was now to give place to the tragic conflicts of all time. The story was to return to its simplest form. Instead of the conventions of the aria-opera — the most enervating feature of which was the "metaphor aria," introduced solely to provide the composer with a suggestion for a picturesque accompaniment — the musician was to acknowledge the supremacy of the dramatist. Standardized sentiment, polite "delicacy," the avoidance of all vivid expression, the bloodless idealization of the characters — all this was to give way to living figures. The traditional plot, in the case of Metastasio chiefly concerned with love and tragically helpless heroism, was to yield to genuine passions.

Gluck's greatness lies not in the fact that he made these demands, but in the way in which as an artist he fulfilled them, in the importance he attached to the development of the opera as a musical-dramatic entity, and in his realization, at first intellectual and then musical, of the essential characters of his personages. Orpheus, the bard and fond young husband; Alcestis, the self-sacrificing wife; the effeminate Phrygian Paris, contrasted with Helen, the vigorous Spartan; the warlike Achilles; Agamemnon distraught by his terrible dilemma as father and king; the sorceress Armida; Iphigenia, priestess and sister; Thoas, the grim and superstitious barbarian — Gluck saw into the nature of them all and portrayed them with elemental rhythms, virile austerity, and a minimum of purely "musical" music, straining his untiring energies in the attainment of subtle dramatic interpretation. Strong in purpose, in Vienna and in Paris alike he pursued his ideal. How far above the cheap plaster-antiques of his age stand his vivid conceptions and visions of these classic characters! How grand the scenes that Gluck succeeded for the first time in welding into a whole from solo, dance, and chorus! What an art was his in accumulation, contrast, and peroration! He had the power of creating an inner unity that replaced the unity of conventional form. In *Orfeo*, for the first time in the history of opera, Gluck employs accompanied recitative throughout in place of secco recitative. The chorus of mourners, interrupted by Orpheus' lamentations, his descent to Hades, the chorus and dance of the Furies, appeased by his playing until, terrible still, they lay themselves to rest; then the change from this scene to the Elysian Fields, where the orchestra magically evokes Nature translated to the heavenly sphere and the choral round of the souls of the blest; then again the scenes of mourning in *Alceste*, among the noblest in all opera; the excited choruses of the people in *Iphigénie en Aulide*, the Scythian choruses and dances in *Iphigénie en Tauride*, the scenes of Orestes' madness — what inspiration, what poetry, what dramatic intensity are here! Note, too, how Gluck in the overture to the first *Iphigénie* discloses the forces and passions governing the play which are later to be worked out in the drama, thus creating the perfect example of the opera prelude. His triumph was inevitable. To deal the collapsing Metastasian Renaissance opera a mortal blow was easy; but Gluck by his reforms overthrew the French conventional heroic opera as well. True, his imitators inherited little more than the soulless shell of his creations. The great choral scenes, the ballets, the declamatory pathos became more and more shallow in the opera of the First Republic, and in the work of the

last of his direct followers, GASPARO SPONTINI —
who nevertheless felt a breath of his genius — led
to the empty monstrosities of the Empire period.
Gluck never had a true successor.

Modern Instrumental Music — Haydn

At the same time that Gluck was writing the works
that were to reform opera, and opera buffa was
creating its own individual style, while the French
opéra comique and the German Singspiel were just
beginning their history and offering song a definite
refuge in which to try out its wings, instrumental
music underwent a change of style which may be
summed up as emancipation from the tyranny of
the basso continuo and the formation of a new conception of the nature of the sonata.

In the course of its development the figured bass
had not only been a method of performance which
had brought into complete subjection every form
of concerted music, solo clavier music alone escap-
ing; it was also in itself a compendium of the fundamental rules of composition, offering a practical
understanding of the functions of sound and instruction in correct part-writing. It was by studying
thoroughbass that Bach's composition pupils learned

their harmony. As appreciation spread of the theory of harmonic principles on the lines first laid down by Rameau, the continuo sank slowly into oblivion. A new kind of melody, a new style of composition arose — not in the solo cantata or solo sonata, which clung longest to the continuo, but in the trio and the quartet. The idea of the continuo necessarily implied a number of voices which were not written out but were left to the player and depended entirely on the degree of his skill. From now on, each voice had not only to play its part in the harmony but also to maintain a melodic line; both claims had to be fulfilled. The whole texture gained both in freedom and in inevitability, and the play of the voices — now one springing into prominence, now another — took on an altogether new significance. The " dramatic " sonata had come into being.

Its nature was new, the laws it obeyed as far removed as possible from those of the fugue; for while in the fugue the first condition is that the theme itself has to be something, the various motives which together make up the theme of the sonata mean in themselves very little — the interest lies in what becomes of them. While the fugue flows smoothly — its form conditioned by the accumulation or reduction of the voices, its climaxes achieved through melodic-contrapuntal concentration — the sonata is homophonic; the theme it presents is a whole containing its own contrasting elements — separate motives that can be split up — and strict part-writing no longer plays the smallest part. The factor of contrast is most forcibly developed in the dualism of the first and second themes in the first movement of the sonata — a dualism that has to be resolved in the course of the piece. The first theme may be, for instance, energetic and manly, the second melodious and womanly, and we must be convinced by the end of the movement that the pair have been well and truly mated. The whole cyclic form of the sonata, indeed, depends upon the unification of starkly opposite elements.

The first movement was the backbone of the new sonata form. Here a fresh significance was gained for the return of the principal theme by force of the dramatic conflict that had gone before. The second movement, slow and song-like, was given to a quiet expression of emotion; variation form was here often adopted. The third, the minuet, was a practically unaltered survival from the suite and so represented the tradition of popular art. An independent, contrasting trio was inserted before the repetition. In the concluding movement, the finale, the sonata came to be rounded off generally by the rondo. This had once been a "galant" piece much favoured by the French cembalists, who attached principal importance to its episodical "divertissements," which merely alternated with the rondo theme. But in the sonata the interest of rondo form shifted to an artful hide-and-seek — to the dismissal of the theme and to witty, unexpected ways of reintroducing it. As in the minuet, here again, to wind up the sonata, a hearty folk-spirit prevails, balancing the intellectuality of the first movement; for this was the nature and function of the new sonata, to compose premeditated and unpremeditated art — the life of the mind and that of simple being, the problematic and the instinctive, and individual and communal feeling — into a hitherto undreamt-of harmony.

It cannot be said with certainty where the modern instrumental style originated. What is certain is that the fluent melodiousness of opera buffa quickly made its mark on instrumental composition. PERGOLESI, the composer of *La Serva Padrona*, also wrote trio sonatas full of a new spirit and an invention stimulated by operatic melody; and we must not forget Gluck, who was a pupil of GIOVANNI BATTISTA SAMMARTINI, the Milanese composer of operas and symphonies. Just as in Pergolesi's music Neapolitan local colour was characteristically used for the first time, so in the South German, Austrian, and Bohemian representatives of the new instrumental music there sprang a fresh source of unsophisticated melodic invention. In his indifference to conventional limits of expression, in the range of feeling in his music and its sudden contrasts, the Bohemian composer JOHANN STAMITZ showed himself so fresh and vital that he may be considered the originator of the contrasted sonata allegro and the intimate slow movement. In 1742 Stamitz came to Mannheim; from this centre his style and that of his fellow-artists and pupils spread so quickly and effectively that, from now on, the leadership in symphony and sonata was transferred to Germany. Paris — not to mention Italy, where opera was becoming the one and only object of interest — was taken completely by surprise and suddenly found itself quite out of the running with Germany. The French were still honouring in Gossec a happy imitator of Stamitz at a time when at home Stamitz had already become an almost historical figure.

Symphony and chamber music were not at first strictly separated in the new style. Works were written to do double duty, with simple scoring for chamber music and then with added wind instruments and multiplied strings to serve as symphonies. The changed attitude showed itself in the treatment of the wind. In the older style the wind instruments — flute, oboe, trumpet — had had solo parts and were used in contrast to the tutti; but now they had to take part with the rest, to play if need be at the octave, and generally to provide colour, richness, and a solid background. It was a long time before the single wood-wind instruments and, among the brass, the increasingly popular pair of horns — the trumpet, meanwhile, having deteriorated almost into an instrument of mere noise — again won their share as soloists in the symphonic scheme and were again allowed to have their own say amid the discourse of the strings.

The hall-mark of the new style, however, was its characteristic dynamics. True, musicians had long before understood how to vitalize their melody by dynamic means for the sake of expressiveness and animation in performance. But with the Mannheimers a wealth of tone-gradations between extremes of fortissimo and pianissimo and abrupt dynamic contrasts formed an essential effect of their art, which they exploited to the point of abuse and deliberate disregard of the natural accent of music. This was the "Mannheim mannerism" against which Leopold Mozart once warned his son. The triumph of the Mannheim orchestra was its world-famed crescendo, executed by string band with horns. The age of the continuo had in the concerto grosso enjoyed full scope for its own kind of dynamic effects, which consisted of alternations of loud and soft, each with its definitely limited volume according to the tone of this or that group of instruments engaged. Now, in the new symphony, the art of dynamic transition provided the degrees between loud and soft. The whole body of strings proceeds with a thematic segment to rise gradually or quickly from the faintest whisper to a roar of sound, and the tension created culminates in a crashing climax. A new world of emotional excitement thus entered into instrumental music, and this new possession, this elemental means of effect, was found to be the very thing for opera overtures, whence its riotous spirit freely spread to the concert symphony. Neither Haydn nor Mozart made use of the Mannheim crescendo in their far nobler and more harmonious works. There still glimmers in the dynamics of their symphonies the example of the concerto grosso, with its calmer alternations between the tutti and the more gentle groups of instruments. The first true heir of the Mannheimers was Beethoven, who, out of the tremendous tension and tumult of his soul, first produced significance and justification for what with them had been a mere play for effect.

The South Germans, too, and especially the Viennese school, helped in the enfranchisement of music from the basso continuo with serenades and cassations written for outdoor performance. They brought into their works a fresh, clear stream of simple melody. The North Germans failed to take this step towards a popular style and consequently lost contact — until the coming of Brahms — with the march of great instrumental art, although they had produced a leader and innovator in the person of Bach's second son, Carl Philipp Emanuel. Fruitful and many-sided though his whole production was, C. P. E. Bach exerted his strongest influence through his clavier sonatas. This music presents the most luxuriant testimony of the age of sensibility. It is full of sighs, echoes, and tearful effusions, yet in the quick movements also full of surprises and unconventional, not to say coquettish, details. In this he was the pupil of the greatest Italian instrumental composer of the eighteenth century, Domenico Scarlatti, whose harpsichord sonatas, in their wit, humour, and originality, remain unrivalled to this day. For Bach the clavichord was an instrument of universal significance, his sonata a vessel of endless capacity. He introduced into it elements from the concerto and the symphony and, according to his mood, alternated between formality and rhapsody. His sentimentality was a malady of that period of musical as well as literary "Sturm und Drang," which had to be resisted by the composers who were striving towards the new style. The three greatest of these, who all in their different ways owed C. P. E. Bach a debt of gratitude, raised and transfigured the affectation of emotion into emotion itself.

A parallel to the relation between C. P. E. Bach and the three supreme masters of instrumental music is presented by the tentative appearance of eighteenth-century song and the wonderful lyrical florescence witnessed, after a long winter, in the early years of the next century. A little circle of musicians in Berlin, their leading spirit an amateur, first occupied themselves with the revival of song pure and simple. Under the influence of the French chanson they set their faces against Italian formalism and flourishes and pinned their faith to simplicity and a style racy of the soil. Their aim was to return to "natural" melody; in other words, to discover the melody inherent in the text of a given poem. This meant forswearing all the principles of the aria. In point of fact, practically all they achieved was this rather negative program. Before the true Lied could come into being, there was needed first a corpus of poetry sprung from deeper and purer sources than the Anacreontic school, Hagedorn's Frenchified wit, or Gellert's pedestrianism. It was Klopstock who fired the imagination of Gluck and of Hiller's pupil Neefe, and the latter in his turn passed on Klopstock's spirit to Beethoven. Without Neefe there would have been no *Adelaïde*. The true springtime of song appeared, however, when Claudius, Herder, and the Göttingen circle of poets — Bürger, Hölty, the Stolbergs, and Goethe, the greatest of them all — brought back into German poetry the true spirit of the race. From their lyrics that intimate composer JOHANN ABRAHAM PETER SCHULZ learned once more to listen for the tune suggested by a simple stanza and to make melody out of the very spirit of the poem. His *Trost für mancherlei Tränen* and *Neujahrslied* are songs that live on to this day as examples of great riches in a little room. His successors, composers like Rei-

chardt and Zelter in the north, Schubart and Zumsteeg in the south, began at length to mark out the
territory of the German solo and choral song; they
freed the ballad from the flaccidity of the cantata
form and cleared a way for Schubert and Loewe.

Of the three classical masters the one who most
gladly and emphatically acknowledged his obliga-
tion to C. P. E. Bach was the eldest, JOSEPH HAYDN.
To him nevertheless is due the eclipse of Bach's
mere elegance and affected sentiment — one of the
benefactions this great musician bestowed on art.
Only in the clavier sonata, in which Hadyn is not
altogether at his ease, is C. P. E. Bach's influence in
some measure traceable; and even here it is more
technical than spiritual. In his weaker works, which
include a proportion of his sacred and secular vocal
compositions, Haydn may seem a " period " composer, redolent of the pigtails and powder of his
century. But the proportion of inferior works is
very much smaller than might be supposed from the
neglect into which they have been allowed to fall;
while in his quartets, symphonies, and both his oratorios he helped the " natural man " of Rousseau's
philosophy to the freedom of music, and did so
without sacrificing a jot of art or intellect.

Of all the great masters Haydn was the one who
served the longest and most severe apprenticeship,
and in this, as in everything else, he had himself
alone to thank. The son of a poor wheelwright in

157

Lower Austria, he grew up among artisans and labourers, and no one cared whether there were the makings in him of more than a chorister or a street fiddler. That irresistible urge of his to make music he had to nourish upon the merest crumbs of theory, painfully picked up for himself. But his contrapuntal instinct was so strong, his vein of melody so unfailing, that his works pleased from the first and rapidly paved the way for him to the post of Kapellmeister in the household of one of the many music-loving members of the Austrian nobility. In the isolation of Eisenstadt and Estoras, where he was obliged continually to provide new music for his princely employer, and in constant intercourse with a by no means meagre orchestra, Haydn developed the original invention, the freshness and sincerity of his melodic style, and the many-sidedness of his musical form, the things that made him the sanest and most spontaneous of all the great masters.

He worked slowly and circumspectly. His first actual symphony known to us dates from his twenty-seventh year. During the next twelve years his symphonic output — even if we assume that much has been lost — barely amounts to four symphonies a year. Each one of them is a witness to earnest and independent effort and adventure. How easy it would have been for him to take over ready-made forms and any number of details of melodic, dynamic, and orchestral technique from his forerunners and contemporaries! He despised them. What prevailed with them was affectation of feeling and facile cumulations and climaxes — games played for their own sake; but with him, strength and serious purpose and a creativeness sprung from vital experience and shaped according to a secret plan. Instead of frivolous trifling he had wit and humour; instead of their toy counters his coin was the full-weighted gold of thought.

Haydn was already celebrated in Paris as a composer of symphonies and quartets and was nearing his sixties when he made the great discovery of his life — the principle of thematic development in the " working-out " section of sonata form. He had declared his principle to the world in the year 1781 in the six " Russian quartets," which he himself described as being written in " quite a new and special way." With Haydn's predecessors, and in his own earlier works, that section of a sonata movement after the double bar and before the return of the principal subject in the tonic had seldom been more than an episode which proceeded by sequences to a modest little melodic digression and was soon home again. Haydn now made of the development section the core and focus of the sonata movement. His "new and special way" consisted in drawing out and putting to the test the forces latent in his group of themes and thus giving an altogether new meaning and value to the recapitulation and thence to the whole melodic action of the sonata. He began to invent motifs with a view to their use in the development section. Already in the exposition of the theme each part in the quartet becomes independent, thinking its own thought as it pursues the main theme in its transference from voice to voice, and yet not deviating from the subject of the debate. Then in the development the melodic material becomes involved in positively dramatic action, engineered by the composer's superb command of a combination of strict and free style. Here was a new application of counterpoint by which instrumental music won, as it were, its " Third Empire " and infinite enrichment of its consciousness and independence.

Not that Haydn discarded the principle of strict polyphony. He had all along known how to write counter-subjects that were true melodies and, finding examples of fugal movements in works of the Vienna and Mannheim schools, he adopted these with characteristic ardour and spirit. In the symphonies of his critical decade he clearly revelled in problems of strict form — in an Adagio in double counterpoint, in an Andante worked in canon. Later on, when he was absolute lord and master and the strict style his very obedient servant, it amused him to apply it to his most light-hearted movements, to his minuets and the humorous passages of his finales. So did Haydn triumph equally over the " elegant "

style of his century and over its contemporary antithesis, the "learned" style, which during the
homophonic vogue had lost touch with true polyphony.

Then in the decade following the "Russian quartets" he found a fresh source of incitement and instruction in the work of his greatest contemporary,
Mozart. This he assiduously studied and, without
imitating it, he built upon it new creations. His
thematic material now became simpler and at the
same time richer and sweeter. A homely songfulness
flowed into his melody, and he delighted in producing out of the simplest idioms those wonders of
multiform expression characteristic of the sonata
developments of his maturity. This last and ripest
Haydn knew better even than Mozart the secret
of giving to a whole quartet or symphony that
mysterious unity which makes its four movements
seem to us like different aspects of a simple, vividly
characterized being, renders every one of these
works unmistakably distinct from any other, and
convinces us that each finale is the inevitable outcome of the whole preceding musical action, form-
ing its dénouement and joyous consummation. He
himself spoke of "moral characters" delineated in
his symphonies, and his contemporaries thoroughly
appreciated this characteristic content, which they
sought to define by bestowing special designations
and nicknames on different works and movements.

While the first movement of the sonata developed its perfected form in Haydn's hands, the second he deepened with emotion from a generous heart and with hymn-like song. An immortal example is the *Emperor's Hymn*, which he made use of in a magnificent set of variations in one of the string quartets. And what a different thing is his minuet from the mincing or pompous movements, powdered and be-wigged, with which his contemporaries concluded their symphonies! Here he frolics and makes merry, sets dancers' toes a-tingling, and can burst out with roaring humour; but also he can strike those notes of seriousness, indignation, and rage which lend the third movement a full symphonic weight and without which Beethoven's scherzo might never have been. His trump cards, however, he saved for his finales. The wealth of high spirits and wild-fire movement, the humour, and the vital union of law and liberty that are here represent a summit of art where Haydn stands alone. Haydn's quartet and his symphony are a supreme achievement of the human mind — a heritage which the glib epithet " Papa Haydn " has all too long caused to be underrated.

In his two oratorios, *The Creation* and *The Seasons*, the master of instrumental music was greatly influenced by the Handelian model, from which, however, the result was far removed, since in the meantime the development of symphonic writing, the relation of the accompaniment to the vocal line, the new feeling for nature — which in music had above all found utterance in orchestral commentary — and the expansion of opera and Singspiel at Mozart's hands had transformed the whole spirit of things. Between Handel's oratorios and Haydn's came all the gains of music's "storm and stress" period. Haydn conquered for himself the style of his oratorio and its sublimity, and *The Creation* thus represents a landmark in the history of the form.

Mozart

Mozart had not the time for a slow and steady development such as benefited Haydn's life-work. All that is contained of human destiny within the limits of a short life of not quite thirty-six years is indicated by that dreadful descent which leads from the pampering of the child prodigy by the courts of Europe to the begging letters of the last years in Vienna and his burial in a pauper's grave. The vital energy, lacking in Mozart for the shaping of his career, in spite of his keen eye for men and conditions, was consumed wholly in artistic "speculation"; for indeed his dæmon did everything that was required for the purpose of fulfilling his artistic mission. Mozart was the son of an excellent musician who as an instrumental composer represented the good average of his time and who recognized his child's uncanny gifts and did not, at least consciously, misuse them. The boy grew up where South German symphonic and chamber music were, so to speak, in the air. At the age of six he went to Vienna. The time between his seventh and tenth years was occupied by an ambitious artistic tour, taking in Paris and London, where the new, free clavier style of Schobert and the symphonic pliability of Carl Friedrich Abel and Johann Christian Bach, as well as the latter's facile operatic principles, were communicated to the boy. At twelve he wrote his first opera for Vienna; at thirteen, with his mind still more matured, he undertook his first journey to Italy (to be followed by two others) and took his place as a rival in the ranks of the Italian opera-composers representing the latest Neapolitan tendencies. His journey to Mannheim and Paris, which may be regarded as the last of his apprenticeship, brought him into touch with experiments in national German opera and with Gluck's operatic ideal, half accommodated to and half forced upon French tendencies.

Mozart's training was a spiritual process such as only a miraculous artistic organism could venture upon and overcome. The acquaintances with new forms of art and new individualities were the true experiences in Mozart's development, which in his boyhood still resulted in frequent acceptance of influences of all sorts, good and bad, so much so that the youthful composer's style was subject to iridescent changes from work to work; indeed, as a ripe master he continued to take delight in assuming a stylistic mask foreign to him. Before long, however, a complete sublimation and new formation of alien artistic peculiarities occurred, a continual absorption of sympathetic elements. The result was an incomparable melodic richness and taste, a musical and spiritual flexibility, a formal assurance and clarity that has not its equal. This clarifying affected not only the structure of his instrumental and operatic forms but also the inner texture of his musical idiom. Never has the natural strife between homophony and polyphony, between melody and counterpoint, been more completely settled. This most spontaneous of melodists appears to have had polyphonic expression at his command as a gift of nature, for all that its acquisition demonstrably cost him some pains in his youth.

No species of music current in his time was left untouched by Mozart, none is without a matchless contribution from his pen; but it was his work in the domain of opera, symphony, and chamber music that was to be most influential. In the matter of opera, it is true, discrimination is indicated. Most of his "serious" operas fall into the period of his youth, and however astonishing a maturity in vocal and orchestral modelling they may often betray, they are still the work of a boy and follow the unhealthy principle of the latest — the so-called third — Neopolitan school, with its sketchy treatment of recitative, its empty pathos, and, to use a contemptuous phrase of Gluck's, its constant "smelling of music." Then *La Clemenza di Tito*, although Mozart's last operatic creation, was a work thrown on paper in haste and under harassing conditions, wonderful in its certainty of style, but impossible to awaken to any dramatic life, and in fact not altogether comparable in this respect with many of the earlier settings of the same text.

Mozart's most captivating opera seria, *Idomeneo*, written by him with the most ambitious care for Munich at the age of twenty-five and held in high esteem in his lifetime, has been connected with the operatic art of Gluck because of some outward resemblances; but in spite of dramatic choruses and ballet music, Mozart shows in this very work, with its bewitching vocal treatment of the arias and concerted pieces and its admirable orchestral details, that the laws of Gluck's opera had not yet dawned upon him — this did not happen in an altogether decisive way until he produced *Die Entführung aus dem Serail* — and that he approached truth in musical characterization from an entirely different angle. For Mozart, opera seria remained a piece of musical jewellery into the set forms of which he inserted the

166

most precious stones, although for his largest aria forms he preferred those which combine a preparatory slow movement with a brilliant allegro — those, that is, which contain a development or at any rate link up two static lyrical elements. In his best period he produced a whole series of musical gems of this sort, either as extra numbers for operas to which they were foreign or as independent concert pieces. To become a great master of the opera seria Mozart would have required a wholly different development and, above all, a longer life than that vouchsafed to him.

It is otherwise with Mozart's imperishable buffo operas and his German "Singspiele." The former reach the height of their species, and indeed far more than that; the latter have, next to their own value, the profoundest historical significance. The history and nature of both species must now be studied more closely.

Opera buffa was, much like the early villanella, whose fate it shared to some extent, partly the child of a spirit of parody and of satirical humour. The Roman opera of the seventeenth century already, and still more the Venetian, was partial to comic servants who derisively parodied the pathetic events preceding their scenes. Then, at the beginning of the eighteenth century, the opposition to the unnaturalness of opera seria, which had so often formulated itself theoretically and led to its transformation, found vent in the intermezzi that were wont to be inserted between the three acts of a "serious" opera. Comedy with music, we know, has never ceased to satirize grand opera, and as late as the nineteenth century not only did the more refined parts of Offenbach's operetta take sustenance from it, but operatic criticism found its monumental expression and its artistic idealization in Wagner's *Die Meistersinger*.

Satire, however, did not suffice. Of the two forms in which opera buffa appeared, the intermezzo in two parts inclined more towards the figures of the old Italian *commedia dell'arte:* the captain, the villainous old hag, the amorous and duped guardian with his ward and her inevitable lover, and Pulcinella were taken over in all their forms. The most famous and still living example of these intermezzi is Pergolesi's *Serva Padrona*. At the same time, and clearly in Venice quite as early as in Naples, the fully developed opera buffa in three acts took the stage; in Naples rather with popular types with the text sung in dialect, while Venice before long supplied one of the most fertile of librettists, Carlo Goldoni, who began early to transfer his characters and his half-droll, half-sentimental mixture of styles to the opera buffa, since when it has followed all the small deviations of literary comedy without sacrificing anything of its earlier contents. Thus we find in the second half of the century a variegated mixing and juxtaposition of the elements of classical comedy with its guiding motives of disguise, mistaken identity, and recovery, its political and artistic satire, its sentimental family histories, its Offenbachiads, its fantastic displays of magic and fairytales, its ancient comedy of masquerade.

No wonder that opera buffa was not long in taking precedence over opera seria. While dramatically it was devised to bring wit, surprise, and lively change into play, it also had a musical advantage over " serious " opera, which had degenerated into a bundle of arias, in its steadily increasing wealth of forms. The intermezzo already, though short of characters, shows the piquant dramatic duet and trio; but the developed buffo opera soon gains introductions and finales in addition to these: the former an incomparable means of exposition, introducing with musical incisiveness several persons at once in some characteristic situation, the latter tying and confusing the dramatic knot with the utmost vivacity for the benefit of eye and ear. This was opera's third triumph over the spoken drama, although the beginnings of the simultaneous characterization of the personages in buffo opera had long been prepared in other fields. The first triumph was due to song itself, which in an artistic sense is truer than mere speech; the second to the revelation of inarticulate secrets by means of orchestral expression; the last to the possibility of representing a scene at one and the same time with a heightened vitality or, if you like, with the utmost truth to nature, and with the greatest ideal precision.

Not all buffo-composers found this full and ripe form of the dramatic finale convenient. In the work of NICCOLO PICCINNI himself (Gluck's Paris rival), the most amiable musician among them, we find next to it a mere chain of arias, cavatinas, and duets. But this dramatic finale, the prettiest examples of which were furnished by Guglielmi and Paisiello among the Italians, led — as a reward of enterprise — to a new conquest: the unification of the scene by means of the summarizing orchestral motif — at that time, of course, always entrusted to the string instruments. Thence the step to the abolition of the stylized aria, to the opera composed right through, was, or should have been, by no means a long one. Instead of that, opera buffa at an early stage borrowed, in addition to its own forms, those of opera seria, and what it thus gained in musical wealth it lost, one must confess, in purity of style. A taste for fantastic subjects, and an admixture of the sentimental family play demanded a pair of languishing lovers who were expected to offer the public the grand aria with its coloratura ornamentation. Opera buffa had begun by scoffing at opera seria; by adopting the da-capo aria the victim in turn enjoyed its most subtle triumph. By 1740 already we meet in Venetian programs with a separation of the characters into *parti buffe* and *parti serie*, into comic and serious parts, and Mozart's *Don Giovanni*, with Don Ottavio, Donna Anna, the Commandant, and Elvira on the one side and Leporello, Zerlina, and Masetto on the other, historically belongs decidedly to this category.

Needless to say, Mozart transforms what his precursors contented themselves with making into a conventional mixture of styles to please a public that demanded all the pleasures of opera, transforms it merely by his touch into an artistically truthful mirror of human destiny, where scurrility and mirth are reflected side by side with tragedy and supernatural gloom; or else he elevates it into the supersensual and therefore reconciling light of an immortal serenity and grace. In his last three buffo operas, *Le Nozze di Figaro*, *Don Giovanni*, and *Così fan tutte*, for which fortune sent him a clever librettist in the Venetian Jew Lorenzo da Ponte and, in two of them at least, true comedy with living figures and an indestructibly vital heritage of the world's literature, Mozart accepted all the forms of the Italians, but recast them in the cleansing fire of his unique musicality. The most worn melodic coin becomes pure gold again, mere formality is transformed into spirit and meaning. Above all, as a token of tense dramatic life, there is his orchestra — " A mighty number of notes," observed an exalted contemporary; " Just as many as are required," retorted

Mozart — which illuminates the most delicate psychological reactions with unsuspected resourcefulness and refinement, and with its richness and beauty of treatment of the wind instruments marks a new departure.

But the incomparable quality of Mozart's operas lies in the miraculous harmony of the profoundest dramatic truth and characterization (which has given us the imperishable personages of *Figaro* as well as the iridescent picture of the universe and the moral decision of *Don Giovanni*) with perfect musical form. In the musico-dramatic construction of the first act of *Figaro*, in its sparkling first finale, which paints a dramatic and psychological action of the utmost complexity with the greatest truth, depth, and clearness, in that tremendous opening of *Don Giovanni*, that point of equilibrium is attained at which the seeming incompatibles of conflicting operatic exigencies appear for once to be reconciled. How enigmatically simple and just is the characterization of the arias! How naturally truthful and yet idealized is, for example, the sweet confusion of the adolescent's longing for love in the few bars which make up Cherubino's aria and canzone! How each figure in the concerted pieces, from the foremost to the least, the apparently most subsidiary, from the Count to Don Curzio, from Elvira to Masetto, speaks its own language! How consummately clear and bright, and yet so sweet and saturated, is the melodic idiom in *Figaro;* to what half-shadows and burning lights is it intensified in *Don Giovanni;* how subtly is coloratura used as ironical exaggeration in *Così fan tutte;* what a novel employment Mozart still finds for it as a naïve symbol for blind feminine rage in *Die Zauberflöte!* How perfectly do the overtures paint partly the substance of the drama and partly — as in *Don Giovanni* — the opposition of tragic forces!

Mozart's German operas — *Die Entführung aus dem Serail* and *Die Zauberflöte* — have a comparatively short pedigree, which this time points to Paris and London. In Paris, too, the high-stilted grand opera was a welcome butt for ridicule and parody, both for the privileged stage of the " Italiens " and for the later theatres at the fairs, where Harlequin took all operatic topics as occasions for his satire. In the same way a national protest against the importation of Italian opera assumed a parodistic and much imitated form in London in *The Beggar's Opera* (1728). Music's share in such works was originally restricted to modest interpolations of songs; but it grew when in 1752 a company of Italian buffo singers introduced two intermezzi by Pergolesi to the Parisians, thus unchaining a violent conflict of opinions concerning the relative merits of buffo opera and national musical plays — a conflict which induced French composers to undertake a musical elaboration of their opéra comique. Duni,

Philidor, Monsigny, and Grétry were its most gracious exponents and led it near the beginnings of romantic opera. That the old "vaudeville" comedy,
too, was capable of accommodating a greater musical richness Gluck proved with the most developed
and influential of his comic operas — which also had
an influence on Mozart's *Die Entführung* — *La Ren-
contre imprévue*, itself, it is true, strongly affected
by Italian suggestions.

While comic opera reached Vienna in French
guise, companies of German actors began by taking
possession of two downright English pieces from the
succession of *The Beggar's Opera*. A new turn was
very soon taken by the Singspiel, however, when it
came into the hands of the librettist Christian Felix
Weisse, who was familiar from personal observation with the opéra comique, and of the amiable,
cultivated, and somewhat philistine Johann Adam
Hiller in Leipzig. The contrast between town and
country, between pure nature according to the conception of Rousseau and the corruption of the upper
classes, was Hiller's favourite subject and gave him
the excuse to cultivate a folksong-like melody, a
simple form of song, without compelling him to re-
nounce the treasures of an Italianate type of aria.
Here, too, a blend of styles was accomplished when
Mozart, along with other Viennese masters, took a
hand with his freshly youthful *Entführung* in what
was now "German opera," which apart from the

connecting recitative, now replaced by spoken dialogue, coveted all the fruits of both buffo and serious opera. What again distinguishes Mozart here is his warmth and delicacy as well as the sharpness and fullness of his musical character-drawing. What a magnificent figure is that atrabilious pot-belly of an Osmin!

But to all this something new and unexpected is added in *Die Zauberflöte*. Here the Masonic symbolism, which the librettist Schikaneder worked into his crude but effective play of magic and machinery, fired Mozart's imagination to the creation of the secular solemnity of that prevalent tone which manifests itself in Sarastro's tranquil strains, the grand choruses of the priests, the airy trios of the three Genii, and the hymn-fantasy of the Armed Men. The transfiguring power of this music overcomes the trite rationalism of the play's meaning and language, rendering its incidents truly symbolic. The whole of German romantic opera took its departure from its wondrous tone. With this one work Mozart gained for German opera a position equal to that held by the idealistic drama of Schiller and Goethe. In much the same way, with a single song that does not exhibit Lied form as we now understand it — his setting of Goethe's *Veilchen* — he indicated a new and adventurous path to the whole nineteenth century.

As an instrumental composer Mozart is scarcely

less great and important; it must even be said that he was originally and essentially an instrumental composer. Much as he did to extend the work of his forerunners, especially that of Haydn, he yet impressed the stamp of his own mind on every form and species, from the clavier piece in variation form to the symphony. With the development of sonata form he concerned himself less than one might have supposed. His especial affection went to the concerto, in which festivity and dramatic spirit, strength and grace are expressed in the most polished and ingenious manner by the distribution of thesis and antithesis and where, following the model of the "London" Bach, he treated the second subject — and therefore sonata form — seriously. Although himself a keyboard-player, he did not care for a virtuoso's treatment of the clavier sonata, which he cannot be said to have greatly favoured. He much preferred to associate the pianoforte with chamber music and to use it for the richest combinations with string and wind instruments in order to throw a keener light on his wonderful melodies; witness his Quintet for Pianoforte and Wind Instruments, his piano quartets, or his Trio for Pianoforte, Clarinet, and Viola. But Mozart occupies also one of the highest positions as a master of the string trio (although with a single example), the string quartet, and even more, perhaps, the string quintet, much as, here again, he owed to Haydn's example. It is indeed a long way from the earlier instrumental works, with their Italian parading of chords, their rushing passages, their sweet melodic contrasts, to the six quartets dedicated to Haydn, with their wholly German character, in which *Magic Flute* sounds are to be heard already and where Mozart's abundance of melodic force, of form, of artistry is displayed with endless resource.

His last and most perfect gifts to orchestral music we possess are the three symphonies dating from the summer of 1788, which embrace such wide contrasts: the E flat, the most Haydnish in form and content, the G minor, luxuriating in dejected resignation, and the C major, music that rouses itself to luminous, serene, and manly strength. What is foreshadowed in Haydn's symphonic themes, songfulness in the allegro movements, becomes plainly discernible in Mozart. What distinguishes him from Haydn — who after Mozart's death continued to develop the symphonic form still more widely and consciously — is a greater wealth of half-shades and transitions, a sensitiveness to sound that has remained altogether unique and was never again to be attained, and above all an entirely different sphere of emotion, at once sensuous and non-sensuous, hovering between grace and melancholy, indeed often changing colour with a lightning-like abruptness. Mozart draws from a deeper well than the more earthly Haydn, a well at the bottom of which romantic lights begin to gleam. For that Mozartian "serenity" is altogether a very strange thing. Not to mention the famous works in minor keys, only those who know certain major movements of his, such as the finale of the A major Quartet or the wild, disconsolate mirth of the Quintet in D, written a year before his death, and have rightly understood the dæmonic fatalism with which they glow, will see the true significance of the clarity and joyousness Mozart could set off on such a dark background. For them the magical, athematic melodies, which are a characteristic of the later Mozartian rondo form and seem to bid the wheel of inexorable destiny stand still for once, will become a joy that will never fade.

Beethoven

Close though Beethoven stands in time to the two musicians whose pupil he was and with whom he forms what is commonly thought of as the classical triad, his name is in itself enough to suggest a new world of music. Beethoven's whole position in regard to life and art was different from that of his predecessors. Haydn had to submit almost all his life to the old conditions of a musical retainer; Mozart broke free from the feudal order of things only to come to grief economically. Beethoven by force of character and passionate integrity stood face to face with the world, a free man. What he demanded of society was the wherewithal to work unhindered, and he demanded it as a right, knowing how much he had to give in return. He had the Revolution behind him. The great artist was rooted in a great man; nor can it ever be otherwise. Goethe, rightly in a way, called him " an utterly untamed creature," a judgment which he apparently never modified. But the contrary is really true. Formidable though the natural forces in this man were, his moral strength was yet greater. He, the son of a drunken court-musician and a cook, developed the intellect to apprehend not only the highest and subtlest problems of his age — the age of Kant, Schiller, Goethe — but, what is more, intuitively to master them. He never troubled much about conventional orthography, but in his notes and letters occur flashes of intense perception and laconic phrases perfect in expression. One such is the motto of the Pastoral Symphony: "Expression of feeling rather than painting" — a phrase that settles the question of the validity of program music once and for all.

The most terrible fate that can befall a musician — deafness — drove him at the age of thirty-two to the verge of despair and suicide, but he knew he had not the right to leave the world before he had

179

brought forth all those things of which he felt himself capable. Mistrust — worst of all the psychological afflictions of the deaf — ruined his relations with his fellow-men and resulted in conduct in regard to money matters which to this day has left a certain opening for disapprobation. The ageing Beethoven took on himself the upbringing of an undutiful nephew and thereby learned to know what pangs may afflict a father's heart. Throughout these trials he was sustained by his moral sense and his unconquerable faith in God's goodness. Just how far the dark currents of his life influenced his music is a question not to be gone into here; but how the tumultuous natural forces of the man were brought into subjection under the empire of his mighty will, were tamed and made the servants of form and order — therein lies the unique supremacy of Beethoven the artist.

He was as rich in innate musical talent as any of the masters who have been acclaimed as infant prodigies, but his destiny was a development of peculiar arduousness as artist and as man, and he was almost twenty-five before his Op. 1, three pianoforte trios, was published. But this Op. 1 was one in which the nature of the man was declared in all its originality. From the very beginning the urge and tension in him were greater and mightier than in his predecessors. He explores new depths of the emotions; sorrow and passion are matter in his hands, and the shapes he gives them are his triumphs. Sonata form seems to have been awaiting his coming; it was now to grow to grand, to titanic proportions, and to be filled with an intenser life than ever before. Variation form is above all for Beethoven a school of energetic concentration. Again and again he is drawn to it, building on the narrowest foundations structures of the utmost diversity and imaginativeness and bending to the service of his giant will a form that had since Bach's time become frivolous and the toy of executants. How and why his groups of themes strain with so fierce a tension, the reason for the huge expansion of his developments, for the changes he introduces into the recapitulation, the new role he allots to the coda, the diversity with which he organizes the cyclic form, and the significant relationship of the different movements — all this is not to be explained on merely formal grounds. Beethoven's music is poetry. There was something he had to say, the ineffable had to be uttered. The musician, the artist in him, was servant to the prophet.

Critics have divided Beethoven's work into three periods, and between "middle" and "late" Beethoven there certainly came a lull in his productiveness which also marks a certain change of style. But from the very first his treatment of the matter of music had been poetic and imaginative. The works of the first period speak of the young master's delight in his own strength and of a bold, challenging spirit. Beethoven enjoyed taking up another's theme and showing what could be made of it. Haydn and Clementi, in particular, and Mozart too, were drawn upon for this purpose. But many a movement, many a whole sonata — thus, the Trio in C minor, some of the pianoforte sonatas, especially that in D minor, Op. 31, No. 2, the first of the string quartets, Op. 18, and the Second Symphony — point to the full-grown master of the "Eroica," a work which, as a whole, but particularly its first movement, Beethoven himself was never to surpass; in which purity of form and depth of poetic intention are perfectly matched; in which an invention, a shaping of themes, an art of preparation and transition, all of incomparable power and penetration, are only symbols of an interior conception, and this not a mere brutal battle, but the very ethos of heroism.

To the prolific period following the "Eroica" belong works in which Beethoven was powerfully preoccupied with pathos and its sublimation — the struggle with Fate and final triumph of the C minor Symphony; the sense of the blessedness of Nature's peace and of divine immanence in the "Pastoral"; the "Appassionata" Sonata; the profound Op. 59 quartets (especially the first, one of the crowns of his whole life's work). Or else the solution is sought in dithyrambic jubilation, as in the Seventh Symphony. There are also compositions that spring from almost pure founts of strength, joy, and self-dedication, such as the Fourth and Eighth symphonies, the last two pianoforte concertos, and the violin concerto.

Mere tunefulness meant, throughout his work, nothing to him. He needed it, but it was to be fought for, not an obvious thing to be accepted. It became, indeed, actually suspect to him, in the conflicts of his symphonic dramas. The whole nature of his work is bound up with the intellectuality of his art. He laboured hard, not because of any meagreness in the flow of music in him, but because he had to realize to the full the ideal of his vision. He wrestled with a theme in its constituent motifs, he rejected and recast, refined melody and rhythm, until the complete and perfect impression was coined. He laboured at building and transplanting, at connexions and path-making; and at length the form answered to the thought. When Beethoven did not quite attain his ends he produced works, such as the Choral Fantasia, which are like buildings with girders still showing through the masonry. A fanciful idea was in itself nothing to him; the greatest daring in modulation or rhythm — and he was the greatest master of rhythm of all the musicians — was only a means to deepen and intensify a spiritual whole.

Entire freedom was his, however, only in instrumental music. After his cantata-like *Adelaïde* he toiled hard at song-writing, achieving mastery at length in his *Liederkreis*. But his only opera plainly shows how uncongenial the great man found the historic opera forms. *Fidelio* is a work that stands by itself, but historically it belongs to the category of French opéra comique in the full-grown form represented by the operas of heroism and liberation of the time of the Revolution. Since Pergolesi's intermezzi had excited national ambitions for opera in Paris, "comic opera" had sturdily developed, most notably in the works of the high-minded and passionately sincere Cherubini; it had gleaned something, too, from Haydn and Mozart's music. While slighter in musical content than Italian opera buffa (it made shift with spoken dialogue in place of recitative), it was distinguished by a more tasteful choice of subjects and a subtler delineation of character. Instead of the rough humour of the Italians, it inclined to pathos; the action was free to take a serious turn, and strong and affecting situations were acceptable. It could, in fact, deal with matters denied to "grand opera"; its scope was wider, embracing as it did every stage from idyll to tragedy, from the playful to the sublime. Now, the heart of the matter of *Fidelio* is powerfully affecting — the heroic deed of a devoted wife who wrests her husband from his persecutor. For the sake of the chorus of prisoners, the dungeon scene, and the tremendous

tumult of emotion in the duet following Florestan's
liberation Beethoven took on the work, incidentally
burdening himself with various minor characters
(Rocco, Marcelline, Jaquino, Pizzarro) and musical
numbers which were vehicles all too petty for his
purpose. That purpose was realized, in all the splendour of unhampered inspiration, in the *Leonore*
overtures, which with his other overtures — *Coriolan* and *Egmont* — inaugurated a new era of poetic
music. The most daring and portentous of the
Leonore overtures is not the third, but the second.

Creation in the service of an idea becomes fully
manifest in those three groups of works which are
associated by the media employed as by the sense
of the music: in one category the Mass in D and the
Ninth Symphony, in another the last five pianoforte
sonatas, and in the third the last five quartets with
the *Grosse Fuge*. In the Mass Beethoven makes use
of the traditional liturgical text for the purpose of a
tremendous and intensely subjective disputation between man and God. In its style, in its freedom and
recklessness of expression and means the Ninth
Symphony forms an antithesis to the Mass and a
complement. From awe, entreaty, and unquestion-
ing faith the Mass proceeds to perturbation and unrest. The symphony throws a bridge over abysses
of despair, distraction, and fond yearnings to the
goal of mankind reconciled in brotherly love and
certainty of God's fatherly goodness. There comes

a point in the Mass, in the *Agnus Dei*, at which the burden of the message devolves upon pure instrumental music; while in the symphony, out of the orchestral complex, human voices emerge at last, as the final and most explicit utterance of the composer's purpose. The text of the Mass is for Beethoven a means to an end, just as is his high-handed adaptation of Schiller's Ode.

In the last sonatas and quartets Beethoven's language has undergone a change. The five pianoforte sonatas form a spiritual whole. Form and syntax have an appearance of unrestricted freedom; but to look deeper is to perceive the inevitability of the organization and the relation to the whole of every part. What takes place in this fluctuating and heaving world of sound proceeds in the higher regions of excitation, as it had done in Beethoven himself; and the last quartets speak, if possible, a still more spiritual language, Gone is the pathos of the earlier works; it lies far behind us. Once only, in the heart-piercing Cavatina of the B flat Quartet, it returns with multiplied force. Elsewhere when it attempts to put in an appearance, as in the "*schwergefasste Entschluss*," "the difficult resolve," of the last quartet, smiling irony makes mock of it.

In these sublime soliloquies of a lonely soul, ranging immeasurably beyond the confines of his age, the subject-matter tends to become simpler and more aphoristic, but the treatment and articulation ever subtler. In fugato, in his "*tantôt libre, tantôt re-cherchée*" fugue, Beethoven seeks to master a new means of utterance at once more intense and less passionate; and variation form moves to the heights of mystical experience. There is no knowing what Beethoven had in mind to give us after these works — he died full of plans for new creations. For us they represent in energy of form and spirituality of content the supremest height to which music has attained.

The Romantic Age

When Beethoven died, in 1827, music already found itself in the midst of an intellectual movement that decided the art of the whole of the nineteenth century and to some extent that of our own days: the romantic movement. The idea of romanticism embraces such an enormous variety of elements, intellectual and emotional, that it is useless to attempt to reduce it to any simple formula. How otherwise could musicians of such various character and conflicting aims as Weber and Schubert, Schumann and Wagner, Mendelssohn and Berlioz, Brahms, Liszt, and Bruckner be enrolled under the same banner? Each of these musicians possessed certain romantic characteristics all his own, while he was at the same time linked in other ways to one or another of his fellows. The essence of romanticism lies in the incessant absorption of fresh material from musical or outside sources and the moulding of all this into new unities.

There had been romanticism in music long before there were romantic composers — long, even, before the word " romantic," a literary term to begin with, was coined. The extravagant chromaticism, suggesting a world of subtle emotions, of the last masters of the madrigal; the unfettered flight of Buxtehude's organ fantasias; the passionate poetry in Bach's expression of his longing for death; the chiaroscuro of Mozart's harmonies — all these were foreshadowings of the romantic age. What now happened was not so much a discovery as the choice of a new angle of vision. The spirit of the age regarded the things of art exclusively in a romantic light and saw in them all only the dazzling enchantment of sympathetic colours.

Thus almost the whole of Beethoven came to be hailed as romantic. The prodigious power of his symphonic works seemed a fulfilment of the oracular saying of the eighteenth-century poet Wackenroder to the effect that instrumental music was the one true art, a heaven that was to be gained by the renunciation of reality. That was one aspect; but there was another. This generation, hearing once more the strains of old German folk-poetry in *Des Knaben Wunderhorn*, found them irresistible, went back to the land, and invigorated its songs at the sources it discovered in the feelings of common folk. Occupational and social singing gave rise to a new popular song; it was the age of choral singing for the people. Great masters of romanticism, such as Mendelssohn and Schumann, and many lesser men, chief of them FRIEDRICH SILCHER, felt urged to contribute to it. The years that saw the national revival of Germany saw too the coming-of-age of the German male-voice part-song — that manifestation of a longing for national unity and the advancement of the race. Carl Maria von Weber achieved the most accomplished and ardent expression of the patriotic enthusiasm that swept Germany during the " War of Liberation "; his songs with pianoforte, too, are stamped, none more clearly, with certain essentially German features. Since then the musical health of the people has been measurable by the fluctuations in the depth and purity of the song in popular use, upon which the musical future of a people depends. Mystical seclusion, subjectivity, withdrawal from the world on the one hand, and on the other the endeavour to place music upon a wider, popular, national basis — both tendencies belong to the contradictory characteristics of the romantic age in music.

FRANZ SCHUBERT is the romantic classic, the

classical romantic. He is a classic inasmuch as he learned from Mozart and still more from Beethoven, his master of masters, and entered into the inheritance of the classical forms with the genius that made him the rightful reversioner. What distinguishes him from the classic is his mastery in a hitherto unimagined realm, the magical sphere of sheer sound. Here, in the world of pure sound in which they live and move, is the ground common to all the true romantics; here is the bond that links them, the clue to their obscure relationships. Schubert led a middle-class life in a quiet, unpretentious circle. The tragedy of his terribly brief career was that life and the world denied him the activities that might have brought him to full consciousness of his powers; but the smug Vienna of his time was anything but the place for that. So it is that Schubert the instrumental composer lacks Beethoven's virile, masterful power. Instead of motifs that actively work to build up subjects and make possible the drama of coherent development sections, he is content with rounded, self-contained melodies and often with amiable episodes that are mere interpolations, leading nowhere but whence they came. His sonata form can often be found fault with for excessive expansion and mere melodiousness, for lack of concentration and all that Schumann, Schubert's rediscoverer and worshipper, called "heavenly lengths." Often, but not always. Not even Beethoven himself achieved anything more striking or more terse than the volcanic climax of the first movement of the Symphony in B minor. For that matter, Schubert's apparent failings are only the reverse side of his immortal greatness. His thoughts seem to spring from the primal fount of sound and melody. While in his dances, waltzes and *Ländler*, his écossaises and marches, Schubert the folk-singer pours out the soul of the Lower Austrian homeland, the great Schubert strikes his lyre as the greatest of all nature-musicians and pantheists. To this great Schubert belong the Symphony in B minor, that incomparable song of sorrow which we wrong by calling it "Unfinished"; the great C major, with its tremendous trombone calls in the first movement, a symphony that declares Schubert to be Beethoven's peer; the String Quintet in C, the quartets in A minor and D minor; the Octet; some of the pianoforte sonatas. In other works, such as the pianoforte trios and the "Trout" Quintet, he inclines to embrace the lighter tones of easy-going Viennese virtuosity. But always he is the inexhaustible melodist, rich beyond reckoning in feeling and fancy, in tone and colour, in the art of his magical veerings between major and minor, and in the discovery by his modulations of depths of the soul never plumbed before.

Schubert's songs, however, are his peculiar glory. Here is the vital centre of his creative work. Who would understand his instrumental music must first know Schubert the lyricist. In the use he made of themes from his own songs (rarely from another's) for the variations which not seldom take the place of a slow movement in his sonatas is to be seen an obvious connexion, but there are others, and deeper ones by far.

Schubert composed many accompanied and unaccompanied part-songs for male and mixed voices, in which there is music of wonderful quality; but his real mission was to be master of the song for solo voice and pianoforte, the German song, the Lied, which is so much his creation and Germany's possession that other nations have hardly or not at all an equivalent even for the name. It is all his own, and is at the same time remarkably related to folksong. So are wild rose and garden rose akin. Such a piece as *Der Lindenbaum* from his greatest song-cycle might well return to the hedgerow and become a folk-song again.

He began as a boy of fourteen with imitations of the Swabian ballad-composer Johann Rudolf Zumsteeg, setting to music Schiller's exuberant and vivid poems, Matthison, Ossian, and much else of the sort that excited his superabundant, pictorial-musical imagination. This mine yielded both declamatory dross and melody of pure gold. But incredibly soon Schubert found the song form that was his own. It was his already on the day — October 10,

1814 — when for the first time he took fire from Goethe's supreme lyric art and wrote that "lyrical monody," as it has been well called, *Gretchen am Spinnrad*, his first master-song. This form, the outcome of the relationship between his music and the text, is, to use a figure of speech, not a vessel of gold made to hold a precious content; rather is it to be considered as a line defining a living body. While Beethoven is cramped by a text, it is for Schubert at once an inspiration and a liberation. He can touch profundity in the simplest of strophic songs — take the setting of Goethe's *Jäger's Abendlied* for example. Indeed, only by compulsion, as it were, and for the most urgent reasons, does his song abandon strophic form; but then, with the utmost sensitiveness and a kind of clairvoyant certainty, he finds for the freest flights of his poets the appropriate flowing setting, compact of musical elements. The supreme wonder of his song is the equipoise between imagery and emotion. There is not one in which the mere descriptiveness that reduces the poetry to a bare statement prevails; his pictorialism is always suffused with feeling; his song looks both outwards and inwards, is at once subjective and objective. Between the vocal line and the accompaniment the relationship is never hard and fast, but is one of sensitive flexibility, though the voice is the predominant partner. His simplest types of accompaniment are eloquent, and so it is that he can plumb the depths with quiet utterance and rise to climaxes of supreme boldness and diversity. What wealth is his in the range of his accompaniment-figures alone; what can he not express with the least of modifications! The most splendid of his resources is harmonic — his modulation. The "*weite, hohe, herrliche Blick*" in *An Schwager Kronos*, the sunset in *Heimweh*, the lover's tears in Platen's *Du liebst mich nicht*, and a thousand other audacious strokes of genius — what a wealth is here of vivid images and at the same time of the vibrations of the soul of man! To think of the miracle of human genius is to think of Schubert. From him nothing is hidden; nothing to him was alien, nothing too lofty, from the plainest of folk-ditties to Schiller's philosophic lyricism, from the clear air of Goethe's exquisite and joyous love-poems to Novalis's mysticism — it is a world as full of emotion as of significant shapes born of an imagination not less rich nor less creative than Bach's own, a mirror and a record of his sensibility in all its delicacy, truth, and power. Most mature and most deeply affecting are the works composed towards the end of his short life: *Die schöne Müllerin* and *Die Winterreise*, both settings of verses by Wilhelm Müller, and each a veritable tragedy in the form of a succession of brief lyrics. He exhausted the realm of the Lied; all that the nineteenth century could do after him was to apply to song-writing some of the new refinements of musical style. Schubert has been unsurpassed to this day.

He occupied himself seldom, and then not very characteristically, with a form of poetry that is rooted more strongly in the popular feeling of the northern nations and reflects that feeling with more variety and colour than any other — the ballad. Rediscovered in eighteenth-century England and won for Germany by means of Bürger's *Lenore*, it quickly attracted the efforts of the late eighteenth-century song-composers, who, however, despite all their experiments — many of them curious — with strophic melody and with elements of the cantata, failed to hit upon the combination of resources proper to melodrama. That was reserved for CARL LOEWE. When little more than twenty years of age (1818), Loewe discovered with one miraculous stroke the true form of the musical ballad, rendering it capable of rich variety and descriptiveness without abandoning the ground of simple strophic construction. He had not Schubert's universality, although he also composed orchestral works, operas, and especially oratorios. If Schubert's music sprang from the soul of the people and yet was able to achieve the highest and most individual expression, Loewe's was rather for the people — often indeed merely for the public — and was not great enough to rise above an operatic kind of melody and a mere fanciful descriptiveness. But in the realm of lyric poetry he helped a certain romantic tendency, which we shall meet with again in opera, to find its particular expression — the tendency towards gruesomeness and an interest in the spirit-world, as well as the cult of Catholic mysticism and legend. No picture of the romantic movement would be quite complete without him.

If Schubert is the romantic classic, MENDELSSOHN is the romantic classicist. The romantic is, in Mendelssohn, the better part. Posterity has to thank it for his imperishable music to Shakspere's *Midsummer Night's Dream*, for his elegiac tone-poems in the form of concert overtures — above all, *The Hebrides* — and his setting of Goethe's *Die erste Walpurgisnacht*, his finest choral work; for the elfin, scurrying scherzos of his chamber music, and for part-songs that wonderfully embody the feeling for nature and the tender longings of romanticism. His classicism was the product partly of his natural harmonic disposition, partly of his education, which was more comprehensive than that of the great musicians before him and of a different kind. He was a master of form. He had no inner forces to curb, for real conflict was lacking in his life as in his art. The melodic idioms in which his feeling was expressed have been imitated too much and therefore cheapened. But his instrumental and vocal works alike are masterpieces of refinement, lightness, clarity, and control.

196

Moreover, in Mendelssohn there appeared for the first time in romantic music the material elements of earlier music — historical re-creation. Just as romanticism in literature and in the pictorial and plastic arts rediscovered the Middle Ages, so in music it steeped itself in the mysterious art of Palestrina. It was Mendelssohn himself who brought Bach's *St. Matthew Passion* to life again after a century's sleep. He admitted into his music the powerful simplicity and the contrapuntal style of Handel and Bach — without, it must be said, being able to assimilate it. He had to suffer it as a foreign element in his musical language, as, too, he merely adopted Beethoven's sonata form, without replenishing or renewing it. Similarly his two chief works, *St. Paul* and *Elijah*, remain in style and intention the witness of a compromise. Yet to him belongs the honour of having been the first to face the responsibility that music's great past imposed — a difficult problem, and one that hardly any serious composer could any longer evade. At this time KARL PROSKE visited Italy to collect the finest of the old Italian Masses and motets as an example to set before the composers of the degenerate sacred music of the age; and a romantic monarch on a Protestant throne, Friedrich Wilhelm IV, took an interest in Catholic music. The eighteenth century had indeed begun to study the works of the past scientifically, but from a merely antiquarian point of view. Modern musicology is to a great extent a child of the romantic movement. It regarded itself in Mendelssohn's time as a servant of art and, full of enthusiasm, turned especially to the supposedly pure a-cappella music of the sixteenth century. Only in its second period did musicology thoroughly justify its existence as an independent science and attempt to shed light on the darkness of the past, to sift material, and by means of reprints to save what was in danger of oblivion. Since then the danger has been that living music might become over-saturated in history. The bond between science and art will only be properly established when, instead of imitation of earlier forms, the principles of the great composers are recognized and from that recognition springs creative art.

While Mendelssohn's extraordinarily early maturity determined his career from the very beginning, it was not until comparatively late and after conflicts and doubt that ROBERT SCHUMANN arrived at music. That may have been a disadvantage for the musician, but it was an immeasurable advantage for the romantic tone-poet. It is a tenet of romanticism that the formal realization of all the arts converges on an invisible centre; and so it was that with the romantic movement there appeared for the first time those dual talents which, if one of them does not preponderate definitely over the other or if they are not, as in Richard Wagner, trained with tremendous energy to a single end, can destroy their possessors. The musician who was nothing more than a musician disappeared with the romantic movement. The fanciful or fantastical standard-bearer of the whole movement in Germany, E. T. A. Hoffmann, was at once painter, musician, and poet. As a poet he gave almost exhaustive expression to the longing and desire not only of the first, naïve romanticism but also of the second, the so-called new, romanticism; while as a musician he had to content himself with imitating Mozart. As a poet, however, his influence on Schumann and Wagner was very great. These two represented, in different directions, the musical fulfilment of what he had foreseen and hoped for.

Schumann began as the youthful champion of romanticism. He found the musical world, shortly after the death of Beethoven and Schubert, whom he worshipped, sunk in the feebleness and self-satisfaction of the Restoration period — in opera, partly in the superficial, sensuous melody of Rossini and his imitators, partly in the unscrupulous " grand " Parisian style; in chamber and concert music, in the empty virtuosity of the Parisian or Viennese schools; in musical criticism, in pedantic formalism. Then he founded, at the age of twenty-five, the *Neue Zeitschrift für Musik*, in which with truly creative and poetical criticism he accorded the great masters of the past their due, and cut a path for all that he discovered that was new, fresh, and original. Thus he introduced Chopin and Berlioz into Germany as effectually as he gave vent to his hatred for Meyerbeer's repulsive operatic humbug. Pianistic virtuosity he defeated with its own weapons. His earliest and finest works — and he wrote, until his Op. 23, only for the pianoforte — present technical problems at least as difficult as those of the virtuosos; but in his music technique is the servant of a richly fertile poetic imagination. The exuberant and rapturous emotional world of Jean Paul, the fantastical dream-world of E. T. A. Hoffmann, find expression in his "program music." Here is an alternation and repetition of minute images, woven out of spirited dance and tender song, hovering between profound seriousness and pointed robust humour, between graceful charm and a "smiling through tears," made one through a mysterious poetical bond and full of secret allusions. And all this is clothed in a wonderfully rich and subtle pianoforte style, which now dissolves the melody in arabesque, now plunges it into a middle voice, now sets it dancing on the peak of the figuration or scurrying through all the voices. It was the new and perfect form and technique of a new poetic-musical ideal.

From the pianoforte Schumann went on to the conquest first of the Lied and of chamber music, then of the orchestra and chorus. There lived in him not only the subjective disciple of Jean Paul; he felt, too, an urge towards great art, together with the romantic consciousness of the duty of cultivating a connexion between art and the home. If he did not achieve his object, the insidious illness which had threatened him already as a youth and which caused his premature death must be held responsible. Or did the feeling that he had imposed too great a strain on his creative powers cripple his imagination? In each of the fields of music into which he ventured, his first essay was almost always the most success-ful. His first songs, in which his exuberant but also shy and tender nature reveals itself in the character-istic postludes of the accompaniment, are also his best, and best of all are those in which he was in-spired by poetry of so genuinely romantic a nature as Eichendorff's, or where he gives melodic expres-sion to his own vigorous folksong-like vein. His first great choral work, *Paradies und Peri* — " an orato-rio, not for a prayer-meeting, but for cheerful peo-ple " — is his most accomplished. How strong a contrast this forms to Mendelssohn, to whom he, so much the freer, the more original and historically more significant genius, humbly looked up! Only in chamber music and in symphony could he put be-side his glorious early works others of later years that equalled them — in the one category the D minor Trio beside the non-classical string quartets, with their extreme simplification of form, and the superb pianoforte quintet; in the other, beside the

B flat and D minor symphonies the *Manfred* music, in which the elective affinity of two spirits of lofty aspiration brought to being a work of true genius. Only in opera was he unfortunate; here another and a greater was to fulfil the ideal of romanticism. And to opera, towards which not merely musical romanticism but the whole movement was striving, there to find its " redemption," we must now turn.

Romantic Opera

The material of romantic opera had long been available. In French opéra comique, in opera buffa, in the German Singspiel, and notably in the Singspiel's coarse base-born brother the fairy pantomime (Zauberposse), all its elements were latent. There had been a number of attempts made in the eighteenth century to create a German national opera, for instance by IGNAZ HOLZBAUER on a German historical subject, and by ANTON SCHWEITZER on affecting texts by Wieland, dealing with classical antiquity and mediæval England. The result, however, was little more than Italian opera performed in German. The movement received its vital impetus from the German romantic spirit, which had owed nothing to these experiments, but much to Gluck, to the Mozart of *Don Giovanni* and *Die Zauber-flöte*, and to the whole of Beethoven.

What do we mean by the romantic spirit of opera? In the first place it was a question of subject-matter. In spite of the respect felt for Gluck, there set in a revulsion from classical antiquity and with it a growing taste for folklore. Quite a new idea of "wonder" was conceived. In the older opera it had merely meant fantasy and surprise, an opportunity for stage engineers; in romantic opera it became the moving spirit in everything that happened. Legend and superstition provided a world of marvels, filling the air and exerting horrifying or beneficent influences upon human destinies. All nature's secret forces took on an individual life and were more or less personified. E. T. A. Hoffmann was the first in the field with his opera *Undine*, based on Fouqué's ingenuous, pathetic fairy-tale, and in the demoniacal spirit Kühleborn created its typical character. Almost simultaneously Louis Spohr tackled the subject of Faust and arrested the attention of his contemporaries particularly with the note he struck in the Witches' Dance. The actual birth of romantic opera, however, must be held to date from the creation of a master musician who by force of a peculiarly sensuous quality in his melodic style was from the outset something more than a mere follower of Mozart. I refer to Carl Maria von Weber and his *Freischütz*.

Hoffmann was right in saying, after the first indescribably exciting performance of this work in Berlin in 1821, that since Mozart's time there had been two outstanding achievements in German opera, Beethoven's *Fidelio* and this *Freischütz*. Here, in *Der Freischütz*, the musician's art is no longer merely draughtsmanship; it is also colouring. Here the German woodland comes to life with all its magic in the horn music of the huntsmen's choruses and all its eeriness in the evocation of the haunted glen; here a born dramatist breathed abounding life into the girlish figures of Agathe and Ännchen (the latter a portrait of the composer's wife), into the weak-willed young huntsman — a truly tragic figure, this — and, above all, created with a couple of strokes of genius the character of Caspar, "the monster," in Beethoven's words, "that stands there like a house." But *Der Freischütz* was in point of form only a Singspiel. Weber had higher ambitions. *Euryanthe* represents his endeavour to establish "grand romantic opera," the German equivalent of opera seria. The worthy Spohr, an ever enterprising if not always successful innovator, had anticipated him in this with his noble *Jessonda;* nevertheless the historic point of departure is the "programmatic" purpose of *Euryanthe*. That purpose Weber himself put into words in answer to a proposal from Breslau for a concert performance of the work. "*Euryanthe*," he said, "is a dramatic essay, counting upon the collaboration of all the sister arts for its effect, and assuredly ineffectual if deprived of their assistance." And again on an occasion when it was suggested that the opera might be improved by cuts: "With so organic a whole as a grand opera must be, to make excisions is excessively difficult when the composer has thoroughly thought out his work."

The problem of the unity of opera was Weber's preoccupation, and the efforts it cost him are obvious when we compare *Euryanthe* with *Der Freischütz;* but the result of those efforts was to make plain the way for the greatest of his successors. Weber employed various means of unification. Recitatives, linking the formal numbers of the opera, were in Weber so much enriched in melodiousness, in expressive power, and in the accompanying orchestral commentary as to undermine the prevailing system of set pieces. Yet more effective and radical as a means towards melodic consistency was the use of recurring musical ideas at dramatically significant points, in both the vocal and the orchestral parts. Gluck and Mozart had already employed unifying basic motifs, in the finer sense of the word, to characterize their personages; Cherubini in *Les Deux Journées* had made important use of a motif for associative and evocative effect, and Weber had done the same thing several times with great subtlety in *Der Freischütz*, the finest example oc-

curring in the Wolf's Glen music, when the hapless
marksman shakes off his last misgivings before com-
mitting his mad act, to the strains from the orchestra
of the peasants' mocking chorus. But in *Euryanthe*
this principle was much more deliberately employed, and with the psychological penetration of
genius. When Emma's spectral funeral music — already familiar to the audience from the magnificent
overture to the work — announced in its transformation at the end of the opera that the sinner is
redeemed, the seed was planted from which, at
Wagner's hands, the whole form of music-drama
was to grow. Wagner did more than perform an
act of piety when he began his career at Dresden
with a performance of *Euryanthe*.

The most admirable aspect of the consistency of
Weber's opera, however, lies in its characteristic
colouring. This was a quality with which he endowed each one of his operas. It was derived from
his singular power, typical of the true romantic,
of so handling the orchestra that the individual instruments yielded peculiar and hitherto unknown
effects, while colours were mingled in the most
varied ways. As in *Der Freischütz* the secrecy of
the German woodland and its dark mystery turn
into music, so in *Euryanthe* does the chivalry of
mediæval France, in *Preciosa* the racial traits of the
Spanish gypsy, in *Oberon* the gorgeous fantasy of
the Orient and the fairyland of the West. All turn

to music, which clothes each of these works in a veil of magical radiancy.

Opera in the Latin Countries

German romantic opera came to birth with Weber's masterpieces, but it was still far from a complete victory even in Germany itself and in the hearts of German opera-composers. "German opera" and "romantic opera"—these are really the same ideas. As things were at the beginning of the nineteenth century, Germanism in opera had to express itself aggressively. Thus *Der Freischütz* was immediately recognized as a counterblast to Spontini, then all-powerful in Berlin, and *Euryanthe* as a rousing summons to the Viennese, sunk as they were in the worship of Rossini. There was nothing of this aggressiveness in the "romantic" opera of Italy and France—a proof of its stronger attachment to tradition, in spite of importations of foreign elements; of the more easy-going way by which it attained its form, and of its internationalism.

In Italy there was a rich aftermath of opera buffa, in which the traditions of the eighteenth century were maintained almost intact. This culminated in Rossini's masterpiece, *Il Barbiere di Siviglia*. Opera

seria, however, took on a new shape, and before
long the old type of solo opera was no more. An
Italianized German, Simon Mayr, modelling himself on Gluck, Mozart, and Cherubini, was the first
to make a move in this direction. His imitators, the
most gifted of whom was Saverio Mercadante, proceeded to stereotype his innovations. Externally
Italian opera became richer, but internally even
more poverty-stricken, if possible, than before. Instead of the old string of arias, there appeared a
mixture of arias, choruses, and massed scenes, and
showy instrumental movements. Opera seria now
borrowed the ensembles of its less hidebound sister
form, and the two, in fact, came nearer and nearer
in their musical aim. This aim was simply a more or
less subtle or crude appeal to the senses. The means
employed may have been enriched, but the use
made of them was soon as conventional as before.
In opera after opera the chorus has its regular task,
up-stage or down, swearing vengeance or joining in
a " preghiera " in front of the footlights, and wind-
ing up the evening with a jubilation or a lament,
while the orchestra is allotted insignificant accompaniments or perfunctory marches and processional
music, crude and noisy. It was the era of the first
orgies of the brass ensemble, in the orchestra, on the
stage, and behind the scenes. The Mannheim crescendo, which in Beethoven's hands was a mighty
means of spiritual expression, became nothing more

in the Italian opera overture than a fatuously exaggerated stretta. Only the vocal writing took on more concise and varied forms. The changes were rung on melting cavatinas and a compressed form of the da-capo aria. The emotional expression was concentrated in the vocal line and was enhanced by elaborate *fioriture*. It was a hey-day of virtuosity in song. Only a few composers, such as the short-lived Sicilian BELLINI, with his *Norma* (1831), rose by finer craftsmanship and a nobler melodic style above this dead level.

ROSSINI's works represent this type of opera at its most triumphant. He gained for it world-wide acceptance by force of his truly magical fount of melody. The exceptional singers his operas required — brilliant virtuosos of both sexes, with huge voices — and the business enterprise of impresarios transplanted his work first to Vienna and at length to that centre which ever since Gluck's time had been the principal market for opera in all Europe and the attraction of all composers, Paris. In Paris the new conception of the "operatic" was finally determined; not in the form of the Parisians' own national opera, the amiable "conversation opera" of BOIELDIEU and AUBER, which with its wit and elegance was as unromantic as possible, while not disdaining a tinge of romantic colour — not there, but in the international "grand opera," the first example of which was Auber's *La Muette de Portici* (1828).

Within the next few years appeared the works in which grand opera was wholly realized — Rossini's *Guillaume Tell*, Meyerbeer's *Robert le Diable*, Halévy's *La Juive*, and Meyerbeer's *Les Huguenots*. What it demanded were striking subjects, handsome historical costumes, and sensational situations; it showed no conception of an organic scheme, but only a variety of such situations in a monstrous five-act frame. It required the most arresting melodic invention, but relegated the inspirations of genius to an arbitrary and therefore inartistic whole. It is these " effects without causes " that render Meyerbeer's operas, in particular, such detestable examples of irresponsibility and lack of taste.

In GIUSEPPE VERDI arose the musician whose long life's work was to transcend, though in a very different way from Wagner's, the false romanticism of the Franco-Italian lyric stage and the pretensions of " grand opera." He began rather in the manner of the minor opera-composers who won successes in Rossini's wake, especially Donizetti, but from the very outset was distinguished from these by his predilection for fierce and fiery subjects, the simplicity and energy of his melody, his native truthfulness, and the striking conciseness of his utterance. His ardent nationalism found its most enthusiastic expression in his choruses, which render his earlier works veritable Italian folk-operas. With the works of his middle period — *Rigoletto, Il Trovatore, La Travi-*

ata — his fame became universal, purchased to some extent, it is true, by a more pronounced leaning towards Parisian opera. The great Verdi emerged in the last three works, *Aida*, *Otello*, and *Falstaff*. Here that forceful melody of his, always so immediately telling, and his impetuous scenic art were rid of all dross and were directed to their purpose with utter integrity.

Intellectually and musically Verdi stands as Wagner's antithesis. The vast background — not ground, but world — of Wagner's works has no equivalent in Verdi. With him human beings, tragic or humorous, take the centre of the stage, and consequently the relation between voices and orchestra in his opera is totally opposed to that found in Wagner. Verdi's vocal line is the vehicle of the expression, his orchestra is a background. The result is the immediate and irresistible triumph of his melody and of Latin humanism, as opposed to the symbolically produced impression made by the typically romantic relation between voices and orchestra. What, when all is said and done, is decisive is Verdi's grandeur as an artist, maintained indefectibly throughout his best works and not to be judged absent even from the weakest of them, however stern the criterion; his sincerity, his integrity as man and artist, his love of simplicity, his consciousness that simplicity spells strength. The best thing in French opera after Meyerbeer — Bizet's *Carmen*, with its vivid Spanish colouring and its lively Spanish rhythms and melodies — followed directly in Verdi's footsteps. Everything the Italian opera-composers did after him he had foreshadowed. Puccini's *Tosca* had been anticipated by *Luisa Miller*, *La Bohème* by *La Traviata*. As for the operas of the "verists," they really derive from grand opera, in spite of the apparent break-up of the old formulas; for here, too, the success depends not upon a whole but upon an arresting part — some melodic explosion, some material effect; in short, upon some by-product of opera. The successors of Verdian opera are little works, of no significance in the historic tale, for their composers were little men.

The New Romanticism

None of the composers of German romantic opera who immediately followed Weber inherited his universality, and it is remarkable that not one made an attempt to pursue and extend the path indicated by *Euryanthe*. Kreutzer, Lortzing, and Marschner — these three all represent a mingling of the same elements in different proportions. Kreutzer, the eldest of them and the feeblest, had no particular dramatic pretensions, being content to rely on the effect of romantic German melodiousness. Towards the end of his all too short and troubled life LORTZING took a more ambitious line with a romantic opera in which he returned to the material of its exemplar, E. T. A. Hoffmann's *Undine*. His real importance, however, rests in his popular, or rather middle-class comic operas of a type which, schooled as he was in the more refined methods of French opéra comique, he raised from the dead level of the Viennese popular spectacle and fairy pantomime, not without lapses into sentimentality and banality, yet with an irresistible blend of humour and feeling and an assured mastery of his means. Alongside this poet-musician Nicolai, who sailed his bark in Italian waters, looks insignificant, in spite of the bid for fame he made by *Die lustigen Weiber von Windsor* and although in actual musicianship he was Lortzing's superior; and the Frenchified and unprincipled Flotow is even more dwarfed. The old mingling of tragic and comic personages characteristic of romantic opera from its springs in *Die Zauberflöte* — whence romantic opera principally flowed in two different streams — was not altogether renounced by HEINRICH MARSCHNER; but while Lortzing represents the bright and cheerful aspect, Marschner decidedly inclined towards the sombre and tragic side of post-Weber romantic opera. The weird, the ghostly, the blood-curdling, was his peculiar province. In his *Vampyr* this makes its effect simply as such; but in his masterpiece, *Hans Heiling*, the whole tragic problem of *Lohengrin* is anticipated, and the "*durchkomponiert*" or freely constructed first scene of this work shows a great advance beyond the mere Singspiel or ballad-opera style. Weber's *Euryanthe* and Marschner's *Hans Heiling* and *Templer und Jüdin* provided the Wagner of *Der fliegende Holländer* and *Lohengrin* with threads for his weaving.

Romantic opera was the realization of the aspirations of the romantic dramatist. What was denied the literary drama, principally on account of the intellectual and ironic elements which the poets introduced into it — not even Eichendorff kept clear of that — was possible in opera. Richard Wagner's achievements, his development of romantic opera into romantic music-drama, were the culmination of romanticism — that romanticism which saw in art the quintessence of life, surveyed the world solely from the artistic angle, and lived the only moments worth living immersed in music. Wagner thus does not belong exclusively to the history of music; Wagner the artist is the incarnation of his age. But before the attempt is made at an appraisal of that portentous figure, a sketch must be given of the two artists who are classed with him as representatives of neo-romanticism — BER-

LIOZ and LISZT, both of whom were his seniors and were actuated by similar motives.

In spite of all the differences between them, there is a bond of union between the three neo-romantics, and it links them, too, with Schumann. This is the consciousness each felt in his own way of the greatness of Beethoven, and especially the Beethoven of the last period. Gluck and Beethoven inspired the musician in Berlioz; the singular and contradictory romanticist in him took fire from Virgil, Shakspere, Byron, and the Goethe of *Faust* — whom he frankly saw in the light of Latin neo-romanticism. To his inflamed imagination the classical symphony seemed too generalized and ambiguous in meaning; he set out to give it a literal sense by imposing a "program." He represents a revival, in new and modern surroundings, of the old French national tendency to description in music, discovered long before him in lute and harpsichord suites as well as in opera. Thus, five years after Beethoven's Ninth Symphony he wrote his *Symphonie fantastique*, in which music mirrored a poet's love-story in a series of visions of an opium-eater, passionate or elegiac or grotesque; while his *Harold en Italie* was an attempt to give a new programmatic meaning to the old symphonic concerto. The full orchestra was his principal medium; only very occasionally did he handle smaller musical forces, preoccupied as he was with extreme and gigantic aims. And so with

215

his vocal writing; huge choral masses were pressed into the service of his ideas. He forged anew the poetry of *Faust* and *Romeo and Juliet* to his own ends, and monstrous works came forth, half oratorio, half symphony, half lyrical and half dramatic, all blazing with colour. Similarly he took up liturgical texts, the Requiem and the Te Deum, for the purpose of a colossal musical exhibition and show of power. And throughout these works, as likewise in his three operas — the first the glorification of an artist (*Benvenuto Cellini*), then that child of tragic travail *Les Troyens*, and last the merry *Béatrice et Bénédict*, after Shakspere's *Much Ado* — he was the master of instrumentation and orchestral colour, subordinating all other musical means to that effect and entirely guided by it in the workings of his imagination.

But however subtle and new Berlioz's blending of colours may have been, and however fruitful his "programmatic" idea in suggesting individual harmonic, rhythmic, and dynamic audacities, he failed in the main lines of his symphonic composition to solve the problem he had set himself. The development section in the first movement of the *Symphonie fantastique* might have shown him the way. Here was the place where the themes and motifs to which a definite programmatic sense had been ascribed were to go through a series of actual experiences; and this is what Berlioz sets them doing

216

here. But he believed, all the same, that his work, "quite apart from the dramatic (programmatic) intention," might yet afford "a musical interest," and he thereby gives a clue to the half-and-half effect of its form. The "musical music" in the work is weakened by the programmatic purpose, while the development of the latter clashes with the strictly musical sonata form to which he still clung. Instead of matching his "program" with music of a closely corresponding development, he chose to divide the story he was illustrating into separate scenes, approximating to the traditional form of the four-movement symphony. This is all the more strange since he had created — or at least applied with a new poetic significance — in the *idée fixe* of the *Symphonie fantastique* the germ of a possible development of that sort. The flute-melody of the *Symphonie fantastique* and the viola theme of *Harold en Italie* guaranteed him the unity of his symphonic whole, even though he did not employ these melodies in the manner of "Leitmotive," not transforming them, but only transferring them into a succession of different scenes. It was left to Franz Liszt to take that step in advance of Berlioz, and out of the program symphony to create the symphonic poem. So far as originality goes, Liszt was much inferior to Berlioz, but he surpassed him in taste and intellectual power. Nothing is more suggestive than to compare the two in their treatment

217

of the matter of *Faust*. For Berlioz this was a treasure-trove of romantic characters and situations, in depicting which he quite overlooked Goethe. Liszt at least made the attempt to deal with it in the spirit of the poet, while reducing it to the simplest terms. His conception was a thoroughly musical one, the material taking the form of three characteristic studies — Faust, Gretchen, Mephistopheles — while actual dramatic happenings are only referred to poetically by the introduction of the " chorus mysticus " at the close of the symphony as an indication of the basic ideas of tragedy. Similarly in his *Dante* Symphony he had vision and ingenuity enough not to be engrossed by the mere descriptiveness suggested by the subject. Engaged on such an undertaking as a *Romeo and Juliet*, Liszt would never have surrendered as Berlioz did; he would assuredly have striven to compass the whole drama into some such plastic movement as Beethoven had achieved, in his *Coriolan* Overture.

Liszt's one-movement symphonic poem is more closely related to Beethoven's poetically inspired overtures than to Weber's " program overtures," the charm of which lies principally in their melodiousness and colour. Some may say that his form is all development without any exposition. All the more attention, then, must be paid to the appearance of his themes. Liszt took the principle of unity of motive very seriously — far more thoroughly than Berlioz — and the art shown in his thematic transformations proves what an ingenious " absolute " musician he was. That variety of expression of his, developing from the most economical invention, was to become a resource of prime importance for modern music. But it was the poetic program that enabled Liszt to shape as a musician in this way, and the program gives us the key to his developments. The form of these developments is as various as are his subjects; and whether it is Tasso, whose progress from despair to triumph is related in the development of a Venetian gondolier's declamatory song, or the triumph of Christianity over the hordes of heathendom (suggested by Kaulbach's fresco of *The Battle of the Huns*) which he symbolized by the hymn-tune *Crux fidelis*, or the admirable character-drawing in the much neglected *Hamlet* — all his subjects not only lend themselves naturally to musical treatment but are also, in Goethe's sense, rich in symbolic intention, far surpassing the literal bounds of the " program." Freedom of form, not formlessness, was his aim. The tragedy of the pioneer was that he seldom achieved that firm and finished texture of strong musical ideas which satisfies the musician. We get the impression from these symphonic poems of an orchestrated version of the supreme pianist's improvisations. From the pianoforte they derive the daring of their conception, but unfortunately the improvisation often entails crudity in the principal idea and mere transpositions and repetitions in place of thoroughgoing development and a close-woven fabric. Liszt's free form involves a free interpretation. As characteristic as the Mannheimers' dynamic gradations are Liszt's fluctuations of tempo. Thus in his *Orpheus* we actually find the direction: "Crescendo and diminuendo of rhythm." A tempo ever ebbing and flowing is the normal thing with him; an abrupt change of speed is reserved for an exceptional expressive effect.

The same independent spirit is shown in Liszt's vocal works, alike in his songs — in which he discarded the compact Lied form in favour of a rhapsodic though still, as a rule, not formless presentation, thereby originating the modern song — and in the most extended forms of accompanied vocal music, the oratorio and the Mass. He is both the first and almost the last musician of the nineteenth century who counts in the history of Catholic church music. Nothing was so antipathetic to the spirit of the romantic age as the rationalistic church music of the rococo period and the "enlightened" generation. The reaction went to the extreme of decrying all subjective, individual expression — though it was that of the greatest composers, Haydn, Mozart, and Beethoven — and indeed any kind of instrumentally accompanied liturgical music. From this "Nazarenism," which saw salvation only in a return to the pure a-cappella style of the sixteenth century and idolatrously worshipped the ghost of Palestrina, Liszt rescued the music of the Church. He understood the spirit of the ancient liturgical art every bit as well as did such composers as Ett and Aiblinger, but his way was not to imitate it but to re-create it as a Catholic believer and artist of his century. The fact was that for a modern man like Liszt the old, simple relationship with the divine world had been lost. It had to be striven for anew, and it inspired Liszt to ecstatic expression, except when he stuck fast in what has been called " the historical and æsthetic amateur Christianity of the nineteenth century." Liszt's two festal Masses, his organ Mass, and his *Requiem* are to be understood in this sense, while his Psalms point to his two great confessions as believer and artist — *Die Legende von der heiligen Elisabeth* and his principal work, *Christus*. The fallacy of " Nazarene " composers of church music was exposed by Bruckner and Verdi as well as Liszt. Bruckner is, in his Masses, the direct descendant of the old Austrian instrumental church-music composers, while Verdi was rooted in the traditions of the seventeenth century. Neither found his modern musicianship to stand in the way of his performing irreproachable service to the liturgy, any more than it impaired his Christian faith.

The great virtuoso and the great man that Liszt was also belongs to the history of music. When he was young, virtuosity, which had since Weber's time been on excellent terms with romanticism, was at its hey-day. Paganini represented virtuosity pure and simple; Liszt, Chopin, and Schumann, each in his own way, transcended it. Liszt did so both by the extent to which, especially in his pianoforte concertos and studies, he rose above the ordinary level of Louis-Philippe drawing-rooms and concert halls, and by the high conception he had of the executive artist's mission as servant and prophet of the creative musician. It was characteristic of Liszt the man that he always subordinated his own artistic interests to those of others. Though never adequately realized as such, he was the father of the subtle harmonic conception of modern music, and he stood sponsor to almost everything that was great and new in the music of his time. His historical significance cannot be exaggerated. As for his artistic position, opinions will vary with the veering of the vogue between intellectualism and romanticism, and according as stress is laid upon intention or obvious realization.

Wagner

Just as Schubert is not conceivable as the supreme master of the Lied without, on the one hand, the flood-tide of German lyricism and romantic poetry that culminated in Goethe and, on the other, the influence of Beethoven as an older contemporary, so there went to the making of Richard Wagner a mighty stream of cultural and artistic elements. Classical drama and the subject-matter of mediæval poetry, so dear to the romanticists, and at the same time the heritage of third-period Beethoven, romantic opera, and the achievements of his contemporaries Berlioz and Liszt — all this was grist to Wagner's mill, all this, with enormous energy and consistency, wonderfully assimilating and adapting, he pressed into the service of one purpose, the creation of romantic music-drama, the idea of a work of art all-embracing. For all Wagner's greatness as a musician, the misunderstandings his purpose was to encounter arose from the fact that he was considered and judged solely as a composer. But this poet and musician in one person was, in a yet greater degree even than Beethoven, a prophet. He made use of drama and music as means to an end, believing them to have been so ordained. The different arts which, after their integration in Greek tragedy, had separated to pursue individual careers, found themselves once more reunited in his music-drama. Quite mistakenly he believed the literary, spoken drama equally with " absolute " music to have been superseded by his new synthesis. Wagner felt himself an artist with a mission; drama was in his very

223

bones; it had to become music-drama because music was for him the supremely "redemptive" art, incomparably powerful and inspiring.

The dramatist in Wagner matured before the musician. As a boy he began with dramatic poems and then, wishing to provide music for them, felt the need of acquiring sound technical foundations. This he did easily enough. A few instrumental works of his pupilage, the chief of them a Symphony in C, show his facility in handling the apparatus of music and his skill in obtaining effects. At the age of twenty he wrote his first "romantic opera," *Die Feen*, rather in Marschner's style; then a "grand comic opera," *Das Liebesverbot*, in which he "took not the slightest pains to avoid French and Italian reminiscences." In its tendencies this is a musical document of the "Young Germany" movement, deliberately conscious beyond anything else we possess in the operatic literature of that age. Finally came a grand historical opera in five acts, *Rienzi*, in which Wagner employed all the operatic resources of the century, from Spontini to Meyerbeer, intensifying them to the uttermost. It is as though he had felt compelled to go through a schooling as a composer of romantic opera; he graduated well, proving himself an exceptional student. Already in *Die Feen* an essential characteristic of the later Wagner is foretold in the "redemption" of the dénouement; and in all three of these works of his youth the telling use of allusive motifs shows him already much occupied with the problem of unity in opera. *Rienzi*, with its extraordinary deployment of musical forces, no doubt testifies to the attractions of grand opera; yet, however operatically, a truly tragic conflict rends the hero's breast and is represented in the action with irresistible spirit.

Nevertheless, a turning-point had sooner or later to be reached, and it came with the first unimpeachably Wagnerian work, *Der fliegende Holländer.* The *Holländer* is still an opera of set numbers; it is not without certain remains left over from the operatic past. But what dramatic and musical inspiration there is in the Flying Dutchman's great scene, in the construction of the second act, and in the antiphonal choruses of the third! What a musical unity, this great "dramatic ballad" that springs from the germ of Senta's song! A whole world developed from the impulse Wagner had received from Emmy's ballad in Marschner's *Vampyr.* The sea is the background of the work, and so powerfully is this realized that a prejudiced adversary of Wagner's had to acknowledge frankly that in every page of the score one felt the wind blowing in one's face. And in the immensely deepened and intensified part played by the orchestra — most beautifully shown in the recognition scene between Senta and the Dutchman, and in Erik's story of his dream —

there is already more than a hint that Wagner was on a fair way to arrive at a new synthesis of drama and music. His intellectual power and range were to enable him more and more fully to realize this role of the symphonic orchestra.

Wagner's two other works of this period — *Tannhäuser*, called simply an "Action in three acts," and the "romantic opera" *Lohengrin* — represent further stages in the evolution of music-drama out of opera. Wagner at this time was still considering plans for historical operas, but the conceptions he actually worked out were only these two "ballads" — the legend of Tannhäuser, which he most ingeniously linked up with the saga of the minstrels' contest on the Wartburg, and the saga of Lohengrin. It grew upon him that for music — the pure utterance of feeling — the proper material could only be the timeless, the purely human. The human element in the first two works of this period is the redemption of sinful man by self-sacrificing woman, devotedly true, renunciatory, and divinely pure; in the third it is the tragic disillusionment of a lonely divinity in quest of love.

From *Tannhäuser* onwards Wagner composed no longer by numbers, but by scenes. Self-contained melody was more and more dissolved in a flowing, expressive melos (not that even the later Wagner avoided strict melody, when it was dramatically justified). Out of small units grows the great whole of scenes, acts, the work entire. While the drama of *Tannhäuser*, with the fluctuations of the deep erotic conflict in the hero's breast, surpasses the *Holländer* — it may be said to be the work in which Wagner released himself from his own *Liebesverbot* — *Lohengrin* in its musical expression represents the supreme fulfilment of romantic art. The hitherto unknown brilliance and richness of his orchestra, obtained by novel division and blending of the strings and wind instruments, his choruses (so often the weakness of a dramatic work), as also the scenes filled with purely decorative music — all these are signs of rapturous musical creativeness, announcing that Wagner the musician had caught up with the dramatist and now stood upon the same height.

The period of Wagner's exile began with six years in which the creative artist was silent. This long fallow-time may be compared with the period in Schiller's life which the poet spent in æsthetic and historical studies, to emerge at length as Goethe's peer. During this time Wagner became acquainted with Schopenhauer's works, which presented to him in philosophical form the thoughts he had already in part expressed as an artist or was soon to express. He also learned to know Liszt's symphonic compositions and derived a far-reaching stimulus from their harmonic subtleties. This stimulus has been underrated by some, and indeed denied.

On the other hand, it has sometimes been exaggerated. Wagner seized upon its elements with such a compelling power as to render his harmonic style after *Lohengrin* in itself an original and independent creative achievement. His chromaticism has virtually nothing in common with the commonplace chromaticism of Spohr.

It was the period of his theoretical prose works, in the writing of which he envisaged clearly his ultimate goal and developed from the composer who had achieved the consummation of romantic opera into the creator of the " complete art-work," which was to be represented by his masterpieces, *Der Ring des Nibelungen, Tristan und Isolde, Die Meistersinger von Nürnberg,* and *Parsifal.* Far-reaching though they are and subtle the æsthetic observations they contain, these writings were really written *pro domo*, with all the violence and the contradictions naturally involved in the foundation and defence of an intensely personal artistic creation. But just as Wagner's creative power was ever greater than his æsthetic understanding, so is his work ever greater than his theory. Now, as once before in the case of Mozart, though under vastly different conditions, there again came into being a musical drama in which a balance was struck between the several forces.

In the older opera the dramatic and lyrical constituents had been separated, the former being allotted the "half-music" of recitative as its means of expression, while "full music" was reserved for points of lyrical suspension in the action. Wagner distributed the elements so that musical expansion and dramatic movement proceeded side by side. The secret of this fusing lies in the relationship established by Wagner between the "speech-song" of his dramatic personages and his symphonic orchestra — "the greatest artistic achievement of our age," as he himself called it. This hundred-tongued polyphonic orchestra reveals the inner motives of the actors in the traffic on the stage above it; it utters their secret thoughts, and the things they know not are disclosed to us. The love that is to entangle Siegmund and Sieglinde is betrayed to us from the moment each sets eyes on the other; long before Sieglinde tells us, we know who the stranger was who had buried the sword in the ash-tree's trunk; we have seen into the souls of Isolde and Tristan before ever the potion looses their tongues. The relation of this "sounding silence" to the visible action in Wagner's art is truly that of the inner will to outer phenomena in Schopenhauer's world of individuation.

Wagner himself declared the art of transition to be the finest and most profound that he possessed. "To be understood," he said, "is of such essential importance. . . . This understanding is only to be attained through the most definite and compelling 'motivation' of the transitions, and the whole of my artistic work consists in bringing out through this 'motivation' the necessary spontaneous emotional mood." This art of transition reposes upon the fundamental application of the so-called "Leitmotiv," which was the old reminiscent motif intensified and strengthened. It guaranteed Wagner the unity of his drama and, indeed, of his whole tetralogy. On it depends the profundity of the effect produced by Wagnerian drama, as also the breadth of the design; for these motifs, of so wonderfully pregnant an invention and containing in themselves endless possibilities of development, undergo in the course of the drama an intense condensation, acquiring a powerful emotional content and a symbolic significance which enables Wagner to unite "the utmost capacity for combination" with the utmost clarity of meaning. The attainment of this clarity required extreme care in introduction and exposition, and the very gradual charging of each motif with its expressive power. All the time the great dramatist never wrote symphonic music for its own sake, but always maintained the closest relationship between the glorious orchestral organ of his creation and the drama, while achieving musical effects of the utmost profundity. It is enough to mention the prelude to the third act of *Die Meistersinger*, where in sixty bars the whole of the Hans Sachs drama is concentrated in an irresistible

piece of musical psychology, supreme in its beauty
and lucidity. Not "the wealth of combinations,"
but the spirit of these compositions, their depth and
their humanity, make of them the great works that
they are.

The role played by the orchestra provided Wagner with the means of representing in idealized form
the action of his dramas. "To concentrate everything into three principal situations, intensely compact and powerful, in such a way that the matter
in all its depth and complexity stands out clearly and
comprehensively" — in these words he once defined
a principle of his art. But in practice this was not
quite how his dramatic poems were planned and
executed. His characteristic narrations and reca-
pitulations — Isolde's tale of the wounded Tristan,
Wotan's great scene in the second act of *Die Walküre*, the scene of the riddles with Mime and that
of the conjuration of Erda in *Siegfried*, and Gurne-
manz's legendary discourse in *Parsifal* — all serve
the music in its task of revealing and deepening
the inwardness of the action, and are essential to the
whole.

The language of Wagner's verse, too, underwent
modifications with this new relation between drama
and music. Down to the time of *Lohengrin* the poet
was still wedded to a conventional literary diction
which imposed at times a certain languishing movement upon the music, but now he found in a crisp

and characteristic alliterative verse a flexible vehicle for the new melodious recitative. Not that he was bound by a theory on this point — or at any rate by no theory more rigid than that each artistic problem should receive its appropriate solution — and so in *Tristan* we find a free alternation between alliterative and rhymed verse, humorous doggerel in *Die Meistersinger*, and then in *Parsifal* a return to a more stately versification. And so also, without ever violating dramatic truth, he planned each act to effect a musical intensification, and it is a source of endless wonder to consider how variously he achieves his culminations, how he allows for points of rest, and how, by retarding and recharging, he builds up the gigantic crescendo of an act, of a drama, and of his dramatic cycle. Even in his later period it was still Wagner's fortune to be able, as with his earlier works, to transcend his own achievements and mount to even higher things. After the completion of *Das Rheingold*, *Die Walküre*, and the first two acts of *Siegfried*, a passionate experience in his life opened to him the gates of the wondrous world of *Tristan*, with all its poignant dissonance that heralds the birth of a new era of modern music. Then came *Die Meistersinger* with its new-old polyphony, and an accession of creative power that enabled him gloriously to consummate his tetralogy, not ostensibly only, but also in inward spirit, and then in *Parsifal* to produce the most intense and sublime of his compositions.

It would be idle to attempt here to appraise these four individually. *Der Ring des Nibelungen,* the composition of which was spread over a period of twenty-five years, during which profound changes took place in Wagner's mind, inevitably turned out incommensurable, contradictory, "involuntary," as Wagner himself called it. Only in the course of the shaping of the drama did it occur to him to convert the dramatic hero of the tetralogy, Siegfried, into the spokesman of the ideal hero, Wotan. Yet his feat in welding into a unified whole this cosmic drama of the curse of might redeemed by love, as mirrored in the profound Germanic myth, remains one of the greatest achievements of the human intellect. The peculiar position of *Tristan* is due to the perfect harmony of its three elements, the dramatic, the symphonic, and the metaphysico-symbolic. *Die Meistersinger,* ostensibly a satyric parody of the Wartburg minstrels' contest, is really the counterpart of *Tristan.* The tragic love so wonderfully represented in the one is contrasted in the other with the triumph of humour. With the lovers' comedy in *Die Meistersinger* is admirably entwined a poet's drama, a thing incomparable of its kind, in which Wagner depicts his own place in tradition, the eternal conflict between new inspiration and the conservatism of the schools, and the inevitable filiation between new and old, the music meanwhile exemplifying the creative transformation of old into new.

The enormous concentration that gives the third act of *Tristan* its sublimity should in *Parsifal* have been raised to a still higher degree. Such was Wagner's intention, which, however, in art and melody was rather less than fulfilled. The ageing master's invention failed a little to keep up with the accumulated symbolism. None the less, this last work, too, possesses a full measure of that magic which, more than its philosophy, constitutes the supreme quality of Wagner's art — the magic of the fact that as a whole it never fails to yield something beyond and above the sum of its action and music and of its external and internal drama. Fundamentally it was Wagner the musician who achieved this, and it was the musician in Wagner who conquered the world.

From some of his contemporaries Wagner received unlimited devotion; from the rest incomprehension and hatred — a hatred to which, with the reckless pugnaciousness of his nature, he was always ready to add fuel by word and deed. He early felt the need of segregating his work from the everyday world and its idle pleasures and of providing it with an asylum such as it eventually found in the Bayreuth Festival Theatre. This he did himself, not leaving it to the piety of posterity, and in so doing achieved the greatest personal victory that any artist has ever won.

Brahms and Bruckner

Wagner the dramatist embodied one aspect of German music of the nineteenth century; Johannes Brahms, the " absolute " musician who, despite occasional operatic schemes, was really at the opposite pole from opera, represented another, without which it would have been incomplete. Brahms was as great a contrast to Wagner as he was to Liszt. Wagner often felt that he would have to make a choice between producing his existing works or composing new ones. Further activity seemed to him at times " sufficient in itself to consume the highest degree of vital energy." That he finally achieved both was the triumph of his unique vitality, and he was driven to it less by outward compulsion, as he himself imagined, than by an inner necessity of his nature. Brahms was not masterful, either as a man or as an artist; but it was the same reserved beauty in his works and in his human relations that attracted people to him, while Wagner, who took his public and his friends by storm and demanded their entire submission, often alienated

the most distinguished because they were too individual to be able to submerge themselves in him.
One such was PETER CORNELIUS, the sensitive poet
and composer of Lieder and choral works, whose
Barbier von Bagdad, despite a slight influence of
Berlioz, is a really original masterpiece, an exquisite
blend of lyricism and delicate humour.

But in his constant striving after technical perfection in the classical sense, Brahms stands in even
stronger opposition to Liszt. His ideals lay in the
past, not in the future, and he went farther back
into the past than any of the masters who had preceded him. He began as a romantic, and it was as
such that Schumann first enthusiastically hailed
him; but he very soon felt the need of basing his
compositions on a profound study of the old masters. Through Beethoven, Mozart, and Haydn he
reached back to Handel and Bach, to Heinrich
Schütz, and to the masters of the a-cappella style of
the sixteenth and even the fifteenth century. It was
as if this late-born Low German felt homesick for
the old South German naïveté and serenity; for the
paradise of melodic purity out of which sprang his
waltzes, his Hungarian dances and gypsy songs, and
his folk-song arrangements. His chamber music and
songs are saturated with it, and this it was that made
Schubert so much the object of his adoration. He
based his songs once more on strophic form, as a
simple relation between vocal melody and accom-

236

paniment, in contrast to the Austrian Hugo Wolf, who transferred the centre of gravity in his songs to the symphonic development of motifs in the accompaniment, although he was too good and, in a restricted sense, too versatile an artist altogether to neglect the stanza. An enthusiastic disciple of Wagner, he placed his art at the service of his poet and in almost every case led up to the climax of his songs by a resolution of one of Wagner's beloved six-four chords. Brahms, on the other hand, drew the inspiration for his choral works, the most important of which is the *German Requiem*, from the sixteenth century. In them he employed an extraordinary wealth of early musical expressive idiom, shaping it successively to his own purpose. The Bible being his highest source of verbal inspiration, he aimed at giving a monumental character to folkart, and in his last work, the *Vier ernsten Gesänge*, he fully realized his aim.

In his instrumental works, too, he began by an analysis of the past, and his sense of responsibility with regard to form shows itself in his abandoning after a few experiments the grand orchestral form and devoting himself exclusively to chamber music. It was not till the last twenty years of his life that he again approached the bigger medium, in his overtures, concertos, and symphonies. He tried to recapture variation and sonata form for modern art, to realize in his own practice the old ideal of musical construction, to banish everything irrelevant, to fetter but not to banish the imagination, to achieve the utmost concentration of expression, and to develop the thematic material organically and with the greatest possible rhythmic unity. Towards the end of his life Brahms set himself a new task. Technically he had long since reached the same level as his models; for instance, he attains a Mozartian transparency in the Andante of his String Quartet in B flat. In his last masterpieces — in the fourth movement of the E minor Symphony, in the Clarinet Quintet and the clarinet sonatas — he found at last a perfect medium for the expression of his own humanity. But the pessimistic content of these works is no mere personal confession. The master, to whose symphonic ideals Beethoven always remained a stumbling-block, recognized that the age of innocence of the great composers was lost to us for ever. ("How lucky those old giants were; they could let themselves go!") He recognized that neither he nor any of his contemporaries, not even Wagner, were of the streams "down which the nations travel, looking into their depths and at the heavenly sunlight they reflect."

But while the romantic-antiromantic movement which had begun with Mendelssohn and Schumann was again drawing to a close in the work of the classic of the classicists, Brahms, who had infused new life into forms which the romantics had weakened and reduced to mere formalism, there arose in the domain of the symphony another romantic of the first order, Anton Bruckner. A romantic in so far as he made pure sound the basis of his symphonies, and thereby produced his most harmonious work in his Fourth Symphony, which depends almost entirely on beauty of sound; a symphonist also, whose nine symphonies, in contradistinction to those of Brahms (which are really rooted in chamber music), once more attained the monumental stature of true symphony. Of the four sources of his musical expression — Bach, Beethoven, Schubert, Wagner — the Schubertian certainly flows most abundantly in his symphonies. He had the same spring of primal melodic invention, the same breadth of form which, whether in the simple line of his slow movements and scherzos or the somewhat incoherent first and last movements, cannot be traced back to any obvious influence. What chiefly distinguished him from Brahms is the courage with which he again adopts the great Beethovenian adagio form, and his lack of a homogeneous rhythmic sequence in his opening and final movements, which he replaces by a masterly melodic treatment and magnificent instrumentation, nourished by long study of the organ. His symphonies breathe once more a cosmic spirit. Love of nature, piety, humour, and mysticism seek in dance forms and solemn chorales the elements of their expression. This simple, rustic, "uneducated" musician was not a great thinker, but a great and sensitive human being, whose battles had been fought within himself, who had known both doubt and joy, despair and exultation, and who had the divine capacity to express what he·had suffered in compositions rich in invention and primitive creative power.

National Music

The attraction felt by the romantic composers of the nineteenth century for simple humanity, the movement back to the land, the impulse to get below surface politeness to the roots of things, led to the development of a side of the art ignored in the classical period: namely, national music. And this brought into the swim those secondary musical peoples who had had no part to play alongside the representatives — Italian, French, and German — of the universal music of the eighteenth century. Universal music had long before flirted with its rival-to-be, borrowing melodic and rhythmic suggestions; thus, Haydn from Croatian and Hungarian folk-music, and Beethoven from Russia in his Op. 59. The early romanticists went farther, Weber seizing upon melodies from Spanish and Chinese sources, while Slav and Hungarian elements were fused in Schubert's rhythms, melodies, and harmonies. Song and dance were quarries for the constructors of national music, the method being for a fragment of this raw material to be selected and for the modern artist to exploit some characteristic feature or another — archaic melody or harmony, monotonous rhythm, or primitive-sounding timbre — for his purpose.

On these lines the greatest master of national music, FRÉDÉRIC CHOPIN, was eminently a modern type of musician. It is significant enough that he migrated to Paris, the hub of civilization. He came before the world as a composer for the pianoforte, and his nocturnes, ballades, studies, scherzos, preludes, rondos, variations, sonatas, and concertos are, as it were, the expression at once of the soul of the instrument and of his own. Every charm of which the instrument was capable he conjured from it; it was never asked for what it had not in its nature to give. Unlike all the great masters of the pianoforte before him and of his time, not even excepting Liszt, he had no unpianistic ideas. This is the clue to his stylistic perfection and also possibly to his intellectual limitations. His age was that of amazing virtuosos, but his own virtuosity was devoted to the service of the most delicate and sensitive taste and poetic feeling. In his melody he rescued the charm and sweetness of the best side of Rossini's melodic

style. Over the light-footed rhythms of waltz, polo-
naise, and mazurka it delighted him to draw tuneful
designs of the utmost grace and tenderness and to
adventure with them into extreme keys, the darkest
and the brightest, through the richest and boldest
modulations, while the old alternation of tonic and
dominant took on a thousand new charms at his
hands. His rhythmic feeling was of amazing sensitiveness, his wealth of figuration and arabesque inexhaustible, and his delicate sense of sound created
veritable poems within the tiniest of frames. None
of his followers was to succeed in imbuing the ele-
mentary material of folk-music with anything like
his intensely personal feeling — that peculiarly Cho-
pinesque blend of melancholy and dæmonic passion
which can range in one direction to a pathological
hypnosis under the spell of sound and in the other
to hyperæsthesia.

After Chopin the whole field of music was in-
vaded by nationalism — song, opera, chamber music,
and the symphony — the lead of Poland being followed by the self-assertion, successive or simultaneous, of the various Northern peoples. Denmark was
represented by GADE, who, adopting Mendelssohn's
romantic classicism, tinged it with a faintly Nordic
suggestion, and later by CARL NIELSEN; and Norway by the sensitive GRIEG, with his harmonic man-
nerisms. The Russian school began with GLINKA
and included TCHAIKOVSKY — though he, indeed,

came to terms with the poor melodic style of German sentimental romanticism — and Finland found a voice in SIBELIUS; England in the noble and sensitive art of ELGAR. None struck so happy a balance between national and universal elements as the Czechs — the lovable SMETANA, who with his temperate use of national idioms recalls Schubert, and ANTONÍN DVOŘÁK, the most inventive and spontaneously musical of all national composers; and then LEOŠ JANÁČEK, the representative of Moravia — in contrast to the many lesser men who emphasized oddity instead of assimilating it, not to speak of more recent musicians who have cultivated exoticism and startling effects for their own sake.

YESTERDAY AND TODAY

AFTER the great victory of romanticism there began that age of transition to which we ourselves belong — the period of what is called "modern" music. This age of ours has two conspicuous features: it presents simultaneously the widest and most incompatible contrasts, and it is also hampered by too great an inheritance from the past. There never was an age when art was more isolated, more completely divorced from life, and yet never had music a wider sphere of influence, or apparently greater practical possibilities of reaching the innermost hearts of the people. And never was there so wide a gulf as between the art of our real artists and that abominable substitute for popular music which is eagerly gulped down by the masses in the musical comedy theatres or absorbed by the aid of the radio and the phonograph.

The burden of our inheritance is felt most severely in the post-Wagnerian type of opera. Not to speak of the mere imitators of Wagner's subjects or musical style, his followers have achieved no more than a compromise between his principles and those of an older day. Some have gone back to set forms, some have laid more stress upon post-romantic sound-effects and scenery; others have made the orchestra supreme, and thus allowed the ancillary art of music to dethrone the drama, choosing subjects that afford opportunities in the theatre for modern orchestral polyphony, with all its wealth of new effects. The composer who has shown himself the most loyal to Wagner's principles and at the same time the most independent and original is HANS PFITZNER, especially in his first opera, a legendary tale that is indeed saturated with music. RICHARD STRAUSS is the most successful representative of the " orchestral " opera. He has experimented with every type of operatic method of the past and has incidentally succeeded in combining a swift and naturalistic declamation with elaborate symphonic treatment. More recently IGOR STRAVINSKY has set himself to establish opera on a new basis, free from all earlier tradition. His *Œdipus Rex*, to a Latin text, is more like a conventionalized oratorio. Other composers have treated opera as a mystery play, as a cabaret entertainment, or even as an opportunity for political agitation, in order to bring what was formerly a socially exclusive function into the atmosphere of the street.

Nor is opera the only branch of music in which musicians have failed to possess themselves completely of the great inheritance. Even the most eminent can cope with only a fragment of it. Richard Strauss in his symphonic poems picked up the threads left by Liszt and Berlioz. He takes his " program " seriously, and can dress up an arbitrary plot with what is undoubtedly music; his clever handling of combined motives makes him secure of continuity and climax, but his knowledge and skill lead him too often into mere virtuosity. MAX REGER, on the other hand, was a great miniaturist; but he could not control the luxuriance of his harmony, and thus became formless (in the strictest sense of the word), and shapeless in rhythm. Almost every composer of our time has been compelled unconsciously to become a specialist in some particular device. Modern technique, with its complex wealth of harmonic and rhythmical devices, of contrapuntal and orchestral

246

effects, allows the composer to make his choice and to simulate a reasonable degree of intoxication. There is apparently an endless range of expression possible between the most primitive and the most sophisticated, so that a man like GUSTAV MAHLER could crowd together elements that he knew to be irreconcilable, and produce artificially the mysterious effect of creative profundity. Mahler knew well the impression made by immeasurable genius, and with this knowledge he attempted a forced synthesis of its causes; at the same time it would be unjust to accuse this composer of being a mere effect-maker, for he was indeed an artist who strove intensely and single-heartedly to find a means of expression that should be valid and intelligible to every type of audience.

Late romanticism developed into impressionism, which sought to induce emotion by artificial means, by the multiplication of minute stimuli and by the employment of effects that are really foreign to music. The leaders and perfecters of this style were the French, whose chief master, both in taste and in skill, was CLAUDE DEBUSSY, as we can see in his pianoforte pieces, in his symphonic pictures, and in his opera *Pelléas et Mélisande,* which obtains its atmosphere with the most delicate and subtle means. Debussy indeed discovered entirely new expressive values for the art of music. His way of treating chords like the mixtures of an organ responded to the most delicate nuances of mood. His subtle and imaginative combinations of timbres have immensely enriched the palette of both the pianoforte and the orchestra, and even his utter renunciation of emotional rhetoric induced in him positive original creation. Debussy's impressionism was a conscious reaction against "Wagnerism" — a national reaction against the hegemony of German music. It was followed by analogous nationalist movements in all those countries which had formerly submitted to foreign domination, even in England, so long obedient to Germany and later to France, as well as in Spain, which had been Italianized. The smallest national units and the largest cosmopolitan communities, such as the United States, have attempted to develop a serious music of their own out of a corpus of autochthonous melody that is often curiously compiled.

Counter to this tendency runs one that may be called "international" — the violent spirit of the younger and so-called "contemporary" music of today. The father of this movement was the Russian composer of songs and operas MODEST PETROVITCH MOUSSORGSKY (1839–81). Moussorgsky's ideal was to write music that should be purely Russian, different altogether from the international music of the West; but his nationalism was combined with a hatred of everything that was conventional in method, expression, or feeling. He aimed ruthlessly at truth and nothing else; he was thus the first musical expressionist. His followers, such as Vladimir Rebikov, Alexander Scriabin, Ferruccio Busoni, and many others, tried experiments with the actual musical material of so-called " absolute " music, aiming at new types of harmony and melody, introducing the whole-tone scale and distorting the traditional chords of accompaniment by using parallel fourths, fifths, and ninths, and so on. This attempt to give new meaning and expression to melody, harmony, and part-writing was afterwards systematically developed into the extremes of free tonality, polytonality, atonality, the twelve-note scale, and even into changes in the basic foundations of music with the employment of quarter-tones and sixths of tones.

Behind all these devices and tendencies lies the desire to do away with all the poetical interpretation of music — or the possibility of it — which was characteristic of the whole nineteenth century. Music is to be music and nothing else. This desire culminates in the idealization of a mechanical type of music which is indeed the absolute antithesis of romantic sentimentality and feeling. The " moderns " regard sentiment as the essential enemy, and the reaction attacks it in various ways. They hate the magniloquence of romanticism, the enormous piling up of instrumental resources, the intoxicating sonority and, above all, the voluptuous effect of romantic music. Even in Mahler and Strauss, the last two and the most sharply contrasted exponents of late romanticism, we may note the change towards a more intimate style of presentation. The chamber orchestra makes its appearance: not a reduced symphony orchestra, but a new organism, to express a new expressive intention. It serves the needs of an entirely new style and technique of composition, no longer harmonic, but polyphonic in a modern way, avoiding homophony and employing a great diversity of rhythms. Mahler, more clearly than any other, stands on the frontier between the old and the new worlds; he displays in tragic intensity the dualism of his time, the exaggerated sentimentality of the romantics and its first repudiation.

Repudiation takes many forms. The most obvious is parody of sentimentality and deliberate triviality, which may range from cheap jokes to the perversion of classical types of melody — though not carried back to the older classics — and of traditional methods of orchestration. "Contemporary" music despises not merely sentimentality but every serious expression of feeling, and its deliberate triviality insults the romantic adoration of beauty, regarding it simply as hypocrisy. It is no mere chance that ARNOLD SCHÖNBERG, who was once the most deeply entangled in this romantic adoration (witness his *Verklärte Nacht* and *Gurrelieder*), initiated the renunciation of the past with trivialities; sublimated indeed, but still trivialities. The romantic wallowing in sentiment is answered most energetically by sheer vulgarity, which is seen most clearly in erotic and barbaric dance-music. Even before the World War — which was itself symbolical of the spiritual disintegration of the world — the tango had come into European music, and in PAUL HINDEMITH's first string quartet the boston plays its part. Fox-trot, shimmy, and rag-time are adopted as elements of artistic music, and finally jazz, an orgiastic dance-music in quick-march rhythm — the most abominable treason against all the music of Western civilization — becomes symbolic of the spirit of the times. Yet even in jazz there lurks a European and decadent desire — that desire for the natural, primitive, and barbaric, a desire that often lifts its head in " contemporary " music. It led Busoni towards non-European music — to throw a sort of veil and mask over his own humanity — and in others it has produced an unchaining of rhythm, joy in mere noise, and the murder of musical ornament, though it has never achieved a genuine unity of physical and mental conditions, the dionysiac excitement of the genuine primitive man.

Barbarism, triviality, and mechanism are all conjoined in the work of Igor Stravinsky. His refinement of barbarity shows him to be more a Frenchman than a Russian. Like Paul Hindemith in Germany and many others, he has lately sought contact with the pure voice of Bach or with the playful prattle of Pergolesi. The Hungarian BÉLA BARTÓK is perhaps the only man who has achieved a synthesis of the primitive and the artistic languages of music. "Contemporary" composers are further drawn towards a type of expression that is yet more remote, remote too from all feeling or illustration, a sort of mediæval gothicism. Through pure abstraction they feel an affinity to the Middle Ages, and hope thus to attain the true spirituality of music. This is the specifically German formula of modern music, observable as a matter of principle in the later Schönberg, whose music has become so abstract, so individual, and so divorced from all relation to humanity as to be almost entirely unintelligible. On this new basis, as on that of mechanical music, Hanslick's idea of form moving in sound is to be realized.

All this repudiation, all this biliousness after the debauch of romanticism, along with the unending flood of merely imitative music and the mild asceticism of the musical "youth movement," is no more than a state of transition — perhaps a necessary one. Whither it may lead we cannot tell. We can only see that we are at the end of another chapter and that music has come to the end of her first, most youthful, and loveliest phase of development. It is equally clear that she can never find salvation in a return to the past, in a hopeless attempt to rediscover her age of innocence. We must now find the way to a new simplicity and truth; we must turn from irony to humour, from caricature to portraiture, from negation to affirmation. If there be still a future in store for music, it must be built upon a new humanization of its resources and its spirit.

MUSICAL EXAMPLES
AND NOTES

1.
PRIMITIVE MELODY
Dance Song from British Columbia

2.
SONG OF SEIKILOS

Ho - son zes, Phai - nu,

me - den ho - los — sy ly - pu; —

pros o - li - gon e — sti to zen,

to te - los ho chro - nos ap - ei - tai. —

3.

ANTIPHON

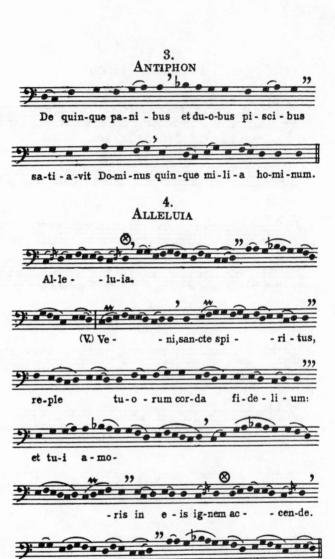

De quin-que pa-ni - bus et du-o-bus pi - sci - bus

sa-ti - a-vit Do-mi-nus quin-que mi-li-a ho-mi-num.

4.

ALLELUIA

Al-le - - lu-ia.

(V.) Ve - - ni, san-cte spi - - ri - tus,

re-ple tu-o - rum cor-da fi-de - li - um:

et tu-i a-mo-

-ris in e - is ig-nem ac - - cen-de.

258

5.
SEQUENCE

1. Psal-lat ec-cle-si - a, ma-ter il-li-ba-ta et vir-go

si - ne ru-ga, ho - no-rem hui - us ec-cle - si - ae.

2. a. Haec do-mus au - lae cae - le - stis pro-ba - tur
   b. In lau-de re - gis cae-lo-rum et cae - ri -

par - ti - ceps 3. a. Et lu - mi - ne con - ti - nu - o
mo - ni - is, b. Et cor - po - ra in gre - mi - o

ae - mu-lans ci - vi - ta - tem si - ne te - ne-bris
con - fo - vens a - ni - ma-rum

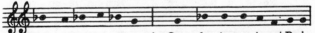

4. a. Quam dex-tra pro-te-gat De-i
quae in cae-lo vi-vunt. b. Ad lau-dem ip-si-us di-u!

5.a. Hic no-vam pro-lem gra-ti - a par-tu-rit,
   b. An-ge - li ci - ves vi - si-tant hic su-os

fe - cun - da spi-ri - tu san-cto; 6.a. Fu-gi-unt
et cor - pus su - mi - tur Je - su. b. Pe-re-unt

u - ni - ver - sa cor - po - ri no-cu-a,
pec - ca - tri - cis a - ni - mae cri - mi - na.

7.a. Hic vox lae-ti - ti - ae per-so-nat; 8. Hac do-mo
   b. Hic pax et gau-di - a red-un-dant.

tri - ni - ta - ti laus et glo-ri - a sem-per re-sul - tant.

6.
CONDUCTUS

Re-dit ae-tas au-re - a, Mun-dus re-no-va-

tur, Di-ves nunc de-pri-mi - tur, Pau-per e - xal-

ta - tur, O-mnis su-o prin-ci-pi Plebs con-

gra-tu - la - tur, Nec est lo-cus sce-le-ri,

Sce-lus da-tur fu-ne-ri, Scan-da-lum fu - ga-

-tur.

7.

TROUBADOUR SONG

Quant li ros - si - gnols s'es - cri - e, Qui nos
Por ma bel - le dol - ce a - mi - e, Vois mon

des - duit de son chant, Join - tes mains mer-
cuer ros - si - gno - lant. Et bien sai, s'el-

ci li cri - e Car on - ques rien n'a - mai tant,
le, m'ob - li - e Que joi - e me va fi - nant.

8.

HANS SACHS (1494—1576)

Morning Song

1. *Stollen:* Wacht auff ir wer - den chri - sten Mit da - uid dem psal-
2. *Stollen:* In geist und freu - den - mu - te Fecht er an es ist

mi - sten Und hört sein suss ge - dön Am zwai - und - zwent - zi-
gu - te Den her - ren sa - gen danck Und zu sin - gen das

gi - sten schön Fru auff den Sa - bath e - - re
lob - ge - sanck Dir al - ler höch - ster he - - re

Abgesang.

Zu ver - kun - den am mor - gen Dein gu - te un - ver-
por - gen Dein glau - ben bei der nacht Da - rinn manch hertz in freuden

wacht Auff sei - ten zu güm - ti - ren Und psal - ter zu hof-

fi-ren Mit gedicht kunstlich scharff Herr dir zu schlahen auff der harff

Mit scho-nen re-so-nan - - tzen Liep-li-chen con-cor-

d anzen Wan herr du machest mich Ob deinen wercken gar frö-lich

3. *Stollen*

In freu-den ich mich rue - me Dei-ner hand werck ich

plü - me Herr wie sind dei-ne werck So gross und dein ge-

dan - cken werck Ab - grunt loss wy das mer - - re.

9.
THIRTEENTH CENTURY MOTET FOR THREE VOICES

Chan-con - ne - te, va t'en tost

A la che-mi - ne-e, El froit mois de jan-vier,

Veritatem.

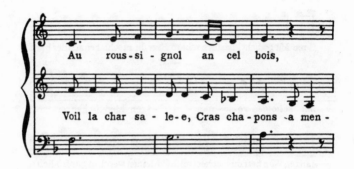

Au rous-si-gnol an cel bois,

Voil la char sa - le- e, Cras cha-pons -a men -

Di qu'il m'en voist sa - lu - er

gier; Da-me bien pa - re- e, Chan-ter

La dou - ce blon-de au vis cler

e ren-voi-sier, (C'est ce qui m'a-gre-e,) Bons vins

.10.

Giovanni da Cascia

Ballata (mid Fourteenth Century)

[*Sempre legato*]

Et que je l'aim sanz faus - ser

a re-mu - ier, Cler feu sanz fu -

Mais cer - tes ne l'os nom - mer.

me - e, Les des sour le ta - blier Sanz tan - cier.

I.V. I -
IV. E

I.V. I -
IV. E

o son un pel-leg-rin che vo cer-
quando credo andare alla se-

- - - - o son un pel-leg-rin che vo cer-
quando credo andare alla se-

can-do li - mo-si - na per di - o mer-cè chi-a-
con-da ven - to con-tra-rio mi vien tem-pe-

man-[do] [chi - a - man-]
stan-[do] [tem - pe - stan-]

man - - - - - - - -
stan - - - - - - - -

- - - - - - - do. II. E
- - - - - - - do. III. Non

- - - - - - - do. II. E
- - - - - - - do. III. Non

vo can-tan-do col - la vo-ce bel -
ho se no'l bor - don e la scar-sel -

vo can-tan-do col - la vo-ce bel -
ho se no'l bor - don e la scar-sel -

266

11.

GUILLAUME DE MACHAUT (1300—c. 1372)

Ballade "De toutes flours"

Triplum
(Recorder)

Contratenor
Tenor
(Viols)

267

tou-tes flours n'a
tès e - stoit li

voit et de tous fruis en mon ver-gier fors
seur-plus et de-struis par for-tu-ne, qui

u - ne seu - le ro -
du - rement s'oppo -

Con — tre ce-ste dou-ce flour pour a-ma-tir

sa   coul-our et s'o-dour; mais se cueil-lir   la

voy-eu tre-bu-chier: Au - tre   a - près

li ja - mais a -   voir

12.
GILLES BINCHOIS (c. 1400—60)

Section of a Mass

271

13.

MICHELE PESENTI

Frottola (printed 1504)

272

mi-ro, ti na - scon-di; S'io ti par-lo, non ri-

Fine

spon-di, S'io ti se-guo, vuoi fug-gi-re!

1. Io ti mi - ro per mo - strar-ti Nel mio
2. Nel mi - rar - ti i tuoi sguar-di Son ad

vol-to il gran do - lo - re Ch'io pa -
al - tra par te in - ten - ti; Nel par -

ti - sco per a - mar - ti Con gran
lar - ti a ben ch'io tar - di, La mia

fe, con gran do-lo-re; E s'io son tuo ser - vi -
vo-ce par non sen-ti; Or se i cie-li son con-

to-re, E·per te vo-glio mo – ri - re; Dim-mi
ten-ti Ch'io ti deg-gi o-gnor se – gui - re; Dim-mi

14.
LUDWIG SENFL (d.c. 1555)
Secular Song for Four Voices (printed 1534)

1. Wol   kumpt der May mit man – cher-
2. Als   das da lebt, sich jetzt   er-
3. Und   sun - der - lich er - freu   ich

lei der plum-len zart nach sei-ner
hebt, der vo-gel-sang, wel-ches vor-
mich heim-li-chen des— ich weis wol

art er-quik-ket das ver-dor- ben
lang ver-schwi-gen was, auch laub und
wes—da-von man nicht vil sun- ders

was durch winters gwalt, das
gras, das grünet schon, der
spricht noch sa-gen sol: wil

frew- et sich gantz man - - nig-falt.
halb ich auch nit traw - - ren kan.
es mir wol, so gets mir wol.

15.

ADRIAN WILLAERT (d. 1562)

Christmas Motet for Four Voices (printed 1539)
[*Tranquillo ma giocoso*]

O ma - - gnum myste - ri - um,

O ma - gnum myste - ri - um

O ma-gnum my-ste - ri - um et ad mi rabi-

O magnum my-ste-

O ma - gnum myste - ri -

et admirabi - le sacramen - - tum, my-

le sacramen - - tum, O ma-gnum mysteri-um

277

281

-mi-num Je- -sum Chri-stum

Chri- -stum, Do-mi-

mi-num Je- -sum Chri-stum, Do-mi-

mi-num Je- -sum Chri-stum, Do-

Do- -mi-num Je-sum Chri- -stum.

num Je- -sum Chri- -stum.

num Je- -sum Chri- -stum.

mi-num Je- -sum Chri- -stum.

16.

PIERRE CERTON (d. 1572)

Four-Part Chanson (printed 1540)

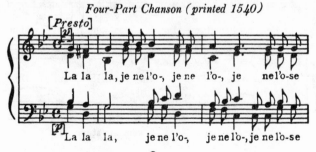

[Presto]

La la la, je ne l'o-, je ne l'o-, je nel'o-se

La la la, je ne l'o-, je ne l'o-, je ne l'o-se

di - re; La la la, je le vous di - rai, et la la

la, je le vous di - rai. Il est un homme en no

vil - le, Qui de sa femme est ja - loux. Il n'est

pas ja-loux sans cau-se, Mais il est co - cu du

tout. Et la la la, je ne l'o-, je ne

Et la la la, je ne l'o-,

283

l'o-, je ne l'o-se di - re; La la
je ne l'o-, je ne l'o-se di - re;
la, je le vous di - rai, Et la la la, je le vous di-
rai. Il n'est pas ja-loux sans cau-se, Mais il
est co-cu du tout. Il l'ap-prê-te, et s'il la
mè-ne Au mar-ché, s'en va à tout. Et la la

la, je ne l'o-, je ne l'o-, je ne l'o-se di-re; La la
la, je ne l'o-, je ne l'o-.je ne l'o-se di-re;
la, je le vous di-rai, et la la la, je le vous di-rai.

17.

GIOVANNI DOMENICO DEL GIOVANE DA NOLA

Three-Part Masquerade (printed 1541)
[To be freely executed, in changing time.]

Tri cie-chi sia-mo, tri cie-chi sia-mo povr' in-a-mo-
ra - ti, Pri-vi di lu-ce e sen-za al-cun con-for-to, e
sen-z'al cun con-for - to, Co-si quel cru-d'A-mor si a fat-to
tor - to, Per es-ser fra gli a-man-ti nui sgra-zia - ti.
O don-ne bel - le, ve-ga-vi pie-ta-de!

O don-ne bel - le, ve-ga-vi pie - ta -
de, de far a - gli or - bi qual-che ca - ri - ta - de!

[with a singing tone]

De, de, u-na e-li - mo-si-na ai po-ve - ri or-bi,
u-na e-li - mo - si-na ai po-ve-ri or-bi - ri or-bi!

18.
Luca Marenzio (1553—1599)

Five-Part Madrigal (printed 1581)

[With tender, dreamy expression]

Io pian-go et el-la il vol-to Con le sue man m'a-

sciu-ga,   et el-la il vol-to Con

pp Io pian - go

Io pian - go

286

le sue man m'a-sciu-ga et poi so-spi - ra, et poi

so-spi - ra et poi so-

Dol-ce - men - te et s'a-di-ra

so-spi - ra Dol-ce - men - te

spi - ra

Con pa-ro - le ch'i sas - si rom-

et s'a-di-ra Con pa-ro - le

Con pa-ro - le ch'i sas-si

et

et ch'i

289

GIOVANNI GABRIELI (1557—1612)

Christmas Motet for Two Four-Part Choirs (printed 1587)

[*Molto maestoso*]

1st Choir

2nd Choir

296

ia, Alle - lu - - ia, Al - le - lu - ia.

Alle - lu - ia, Al - le - lu - - ia.

ia, Al - le - lu - ia, Al - le - lu - ia.

20.

GIOVANNI GIACOMO GASTOLDI

Five-Part Dance-Song (Balletto) (printed 1591)

Speme amorosa (Hope of love) [*Allegro vivace*]

1. Vez - zo - set - te Nin - fe e bel - le Ch'in bel -
2. Questo a noi pro - mi - se A - mo - re, Quando a

3. Non con - vien che tan - ta fe - de, Come a

4. Vi - ta o - mai por - ge - te a no - i, Si le -

297

tà tut-te vin - ce - te Le più va-ghe pa-sto-
suci do-ra-ti stra-li Fè ber - sa-glio il no-stro

ve-te in noi già scor-ta, Ab-bia mor-te per mer-
a - lie fi-di a - man-ti, Che'l mo - rir sprez-ziam per

rel -le, Fa la la la la la la! Vez-zo-   la! 1. A
co - re,   Questo a   2. Or

ce - de,   Non con-   3. Da
                                              4. Quel

vo - i,   Vi-ta o-

voi   chia - mia - mo
dun - que ab-bia - te

voi   a - i - ta 1.Pie - tà   chie pie
fin   sia o - ma - i 2.Di noi   pie-

                        3. Spe - ria - - mo e
                        4. De no - stri

298

299

21.
ANDREA GABRIELI (c. 1510—86)
Intonation for Organ in the Second Church Mode (printed 1593)

22.

Claudio Merulo (1533—1604)

Ricercar for Organ (1567)

305

306

23.

JOHN DOWLAND (1562—1626)

Song for Voice and Lute (1597)

Voice

My thoughts are winged with hopes, my   hopes with

Lute

307

love. Mount, Love, un-to the moon in clearest night,

And say, as she doth in the heav-ens move,

In earth so wanes and wax-eth my de-light.

And whisper this but soft - ly in her ears:

Hope oft doth hang the head and Trust shed tears.

24.

MARCO DA GAGLIANO (d. 1642)

Apollo's Lament from the Opera "La Dafne" (1608)

Dun - que ru-vi-da scor-za Chiu-de-rà sem-

pre la bel-tà ce-le - ste? Lu-mi, voi che ve-de-ste L'al-ta bel-tà, ch'a la-gri-mar vi sfor-za Af-fis-sa-te-vi pur in questa fron-de: Qui po-sa, e qui s'ascon-de Il mio be - ne, il mio co - re, il mio te-so - ro, Per cui ben - ch'immortal, languisco e mo - ro.

25.

GIOVANNI DI MACQUE

Four-Part Canzon alla Francese

for Four Strings or a Keyboard Instrument (c. 1600)

[Allegretto]

312

26.

PAUL PEUERL

German Variations Suite (1611)

Intrada
[Più mosso]

314

Dance
[*Allegro*]

315

Galliard
[*Vivace*]

27

HEINRICH SCHÜTZ (1585—1672)
*Concerted Motet for Voice (Soprano or Tenor), Two Violins and
Accompanying Instruments (Organ or Clavier) (printed 1647)*
[*To be freely executed*]

Der Herr ist mei - ne Stär - ke, mei-ne

Stär-ke und mein Lob-ge-sang, mein Lobgesang und mein

Heil. Er ist mein Gott, ich will ihn prei - sen, er ist mein

Gott, ich will ihn preisen, er ist meines Vaters Gott, ich will ihn er-

he - ben, er ist mei-nes Va-ters Gott, ich will ihn er-

Violins

he - - - - ben.

Herr, wer ist dir

gleich, wer ist dir gleich,   wer ist dir gleich un-ter den

Göt-tern,wer ist dir gleich,   wer ist dir gleich, wer ist dir

gleich, der so mächtig, so heilig, so schrecklich, so löblich, so

wun - der - tä - tig ist,

der so mächtig, só hei - lig, so

schrecklich, so löblich, so wun-der-tä-tig, so wundertätig ist!

[Giocoso e fermo, Andante]

Ich will dem Herren sin-gen, sin-gen will ich dem Herrn mein Leben lang. Ich will dem Herren sin-gen, sin-gen will ich dem Herrn mein Le-ben lang, mein Le-ben lang, und meinen Gott lo - ben, und meinen Gott loben, meinen Gott loben, so lang ich hie bin; und meinen Gott

loben, meinen Gott loben, meinen Gott loben, so lang ich hie

[Violine]

bin,   singen will ich dem Herrn,   singen will ich dem

Herrn,   ich will dem Herren singen,   sin-gen will ich dem

Herrn mein Leben lang und meinen Gott lo-ben,

und meinen Gott lo - ben,

und meinen Gott loben, meinen Gott loben, so lang ich hie

bin, sin - gen will ich dem Herrn,

ich will dem Herren sin - gen mein Le - ben lang.

und meinen Gott lo-ben, so lang ich le - be.

28.

DOMENICO GABRIELLI (d. 1690)

Chamber Cantata

for Soprano and Basso Continuo (printed 1691)

Recitativo

Poi-che ad I - re - ne in van Tir-si il Pa-sto - re Col

cor più vol-te in la-gri-me di - sciol-to, Fe-de giu-rò in A -

mo-re, Al - la bel-tà ri - vol - to, Tan-to ver lui cru-

323

de-le, Contai det-ti a-ni - mò le sue que-re - le:

Aria "Largo"

So-li - ta-ri fiu-mi-cel-li, Di - te voi, se a-

do-ro I - re - ne! Di - te voi, se a-do-ro I - re -

ne, Di - te voi se a-do-ro I - re - ne, Di - te

voi se a-do-ro I - re - ne!

Aria da Capo sino al Fine

325

Recitativo

E se l'au-ra, e se il fiu-me Non son ba-stan-ti a di-vi-sar l'ar-do-re Che m'ac-ce-se nel co-re Il par-go-let-to e fa-re-tra-to Nu-me: An co i sas-si, e le piante Benche mu-te di-ran che Tirsi è a-man-te.

Aria
Allegro

f Quello spe-co ch'è cin-to di fron-de,

326

Quel-lo spe-co ch'è cin-to di fron-de   E le

vo - ci con ec - co ri - spon-de,   Se mi

struggo,   ei ti di - rà! Se mi strug-go,

ei ti di-rà!   Se mi struggo, ei ti di-

rà, Se mi struggo, ei ti di - rà!   *Fine*

327

Largo

E gli oh Dio, che ap - pre - se so - lo   A ri-

dir   vo - ci di   duo - lo,   Dal mio duol

mosso a pie - tà,   Dal mio duol   mos - so a pie-

pp

tà;   Dal mio duol mos - so a pie - tà.

pp

Aria da Capo sino al Fine

Recitativo

f   *sf*

Ne tu mi cre - di   an - co - ra? Ah!   t'in-

328

ten - do, cru-del!   tu   voi ch'io mo - ra!

Si si mor-rò; ma al - men con-ce-da A-mo-re Per mo-

strar che d'I-re-ne A-man-te cad-de Un mi-se-ro Pa-

sto-re: Che al suon delle mie pe-ne, Pianga, ca-da, so-

Arioso

spi-ri e for-mi l'ec-co Il fiu-me, il tronco, il venti-

329

cel,   lo spe-co.   Il fiu-me, il

tronco, il ven-ti-cel,   lo spe-co. *pp*   *ppp*

29.

JOHN RAVENSCROFT (d. c. 1745)

Church Sonata (Trio Sonata)

for Two Violins and Basso Continuo (printed 1695)

Grave

335

336

337

30.

<small>AGOSTINO STEFFANI (1654—1728)</small>

French Overture

339

31.

NICOLA PICCINNI (1728—1800)

Italian Overture

341

342

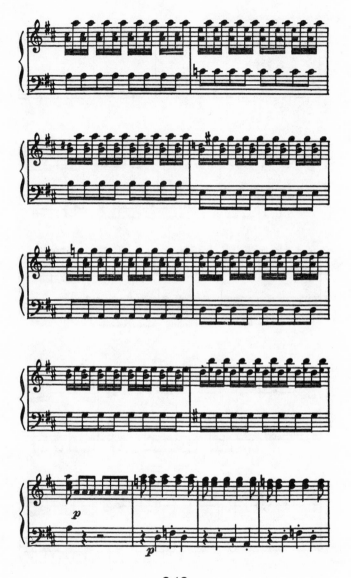

348

349

32.

GIOVANNI BATTISTA SOMIS (1676—1763)

Solo Sonata for Violin and Basso Continuo

Adagio

351

352

353

354

355

357

33.

JOHANN SEBASTIAN BACH

Concerto Grosso (Prelude from the Third English Suite)
[*Allegro molto e con fuoco*]

359

360

363

364

365

366

367

34.

JOHANN KASPAR FERDINAND FISCHER (1670—1746?)

Suite for Clavier (printed 1696)

Prelude
[*Tranquillo con moto*]

Passacaille
[Con energia]

2nd part

Finis

370

Bourée
[*Allegro vivace*]

371

Finis

35.

JOHANN PACHELBEL (1653—1706)

Choral Prelude for Organ

36

GIOVANNI BATTISTA PERGOLESI (1710—36)

Buffo Aria

Stiz - zo - so mio stiz - zo - so, voi

fa - te il bo - ri - o - so, ma...

no, ma non vi può gio - va - re! Ma...

no,   ma non vi può gio-va-re! Bi - so-gna al

mio di - vie-to star che - - to,

che - to, e non par - la-re Zit!

Zit! Ser-pi - na vuol co - si Zit!

Zit! Ser-pi - na vuol co - si.

Stiz-zo-so

mio stiz - zo-so, voi fa-teil bo-ri-

o-so. - Ma... no, ma non vi puo gio-

va - re! Bi - so - gna al mio di - vie - to star

che - to, che - to, e non par -

la - re! Zit! Zit! Ser - pi - na

vuol co - si. Voi fa - to il bo - ri - o - so, ma

379

si,   vuol co - si, Ser-pi - na   vuol co -

si.   Cre-

Fine

d'io che m'in-te - de-te, si,   che m'inten-

de-te, si,   chem'inten-de-te, da chemi co-no-

380

sce-te, son mol-ti e mol-ti dì, son mol - -

ti, mol - ti, e mol - ti dì!

Stiz-

37.

WOLFGANG AMADEUS MOZART (1756—91)

Buffo Finale (Fragment)

Susanna.
tar-mi, qual ri-me-dio ri-tro-var, qual ri-

La Contessa.
me-dio ri-tro-var, qual ri-me-dio, qual ri-

Il Conte.
io mi sen-to a

Figaro.
scon - cer - tar - mi, qual ri-

me - dio ri - tro-var?

me - dio ri - tro-var?

con - so - lar.

me - dio ri - tro-var?

(al Conte)
Son tre sto-li-di, tre

384

paz-zi, co-sa mai vengono a far, co-sa

Il Conte

mai ven-go-no a far? Pian, pia-

nin, sen-za schia-maz-zi, di - ca o-

gn'un quel che gli par, di-ca o - gn'un quel che gli

cresc. f

Marcellina

Un im - pe-gno nuzzi - a-le ha co-stui con me con -

par.

p

p *p*

trat-to, e pre-ten-do ch'il con-trat-to de-va me co ef-fet-tu-

Bartolo.

qui   per   giu -   - di - car.   Io da

lei scel-to avvo - ca-to, ven-go a far le sue di -

fe-se, le le-gi-ti-me pre - te-se io vi ven-go a pa-le-

388

Susanna.

È un birban-te, è un birbante!

La Contessa.

È un birban-te, è un birbante!

Bartolo.

sar.

Figaro.

È un birban-te, è un birbante!

Il Conte.

O -

là! si - len - zio! si - len - zio! si - len - -

389

Basilio.

Io co -
zio! Io son qui per giu - di - car.

m'uom al mondo co-gni-to, vengo qui per te-sti-

mo-nio del promesso matri - monio con prestanza di da-

dre-mo, il con-trat-to leg-ge -

re-mo, tut-to in or - din de - ve an-

Susanna.

f *Più allegro*

La Contessa.

Son con - fu - sa, son stor-

Il Conte.

Son con-fu-sa, son stor-

dar.

Figaro.

f

Son con-fu-so, son stor-

Più allegro

392

393

38.

Joseph Haydn (1732—1809)

Quartet Movement (Op. 33, 2)

Allegro moderato, cantabile

397

398

401

402

39.

CHRISTOPH WILLIBALD GLUCK (1714—87)

Accompanied Recitative

from "Iphigénie en Tauride" (Acte II,3) (1779)

Dieúx! protecteurs de ces affreux ri - vages, Dieux! a-

vides de sang, ton-nez!

Tonnez! écrasez moi!   écrasez

Lent

f [il tombe]

moi!

Où suis-je?

409

À l'horreur qui m'obsède quelle tranquillité succède?

Le cal -   - me

etc.

ren - tre dans mon cœur!

etc.

411

NOTES

1. The primitive melody that opens these examples is taken from a study by O. Abraham and E. M. von Hornbostel (*Recorded Indian Melodies from British Columbia*) which appeared in 1906, reprinted in the *Collection for Comparative Musicology* (Munich, 1922), Vol. I, p. 291, ff.[1] There it undergoes an exact scientific analysis; for our purposes it suffices to say that here we obviously have an entirely simple single-measure motif, in which nevertheless a statement with an apparently upward beat, and an answer to this state-

[1] Professor von Hornbostel was kind enough to offer it to me in a new transcription.

413

ment, are clearly distinguishable. This motif, in which the notes move closely about a central note, is, with slight variations, endlessly repeated, and is accompanied by a syncopated drum-beat rhythm, in which the inciting, orgiastic dance-element of such songs is actually conveyed. The intervals are not pure ones in our sense, but are fluctuatingly intoned. It is worth noticing that in the space of a fifth, within which this monotonous tone-movement takes place, the semitone is not touched, the E is completely lacking. For such an "order" would already presuppose a higher degree of melodic sensitivity, and is here still avoided: our motif is "plainly the embryo of the pentatonic."

2. As an example of an antique melody, former editions of this book contained the beginning of the first Pythian ode of the Theban lyric poet Pindar, handed down to us through the learned Jesuit, Athanasius Kircher, in his *Musurgia* (1650), allegedly after a manuscript in Messina. In the meantime it has been made evident (Otto Gombosi: "The Melody of Pindar's 'Golden Lyre,'" *Musical Quarterly*, XXVI, 381 ff.) that the melody was forged, very cleverly, by Kircher himself.

We replace the example by the only extant specimen of a Greek lyrical poem with music, the "Skolion," discovered in 1883 on a column in Tralles (Asia Minor). It is a nenia for a certain Seikilos: a simple and moving elegy about the transitoriness of life. The melody stays in the (Greek) Phrygian mode, using every note of the scale, with the "Mese" (= middle tone) a flat in the Iastic tuning; slowly sinking from the highest to the lowest tone. We follow the transcription given by Hugo Riemann in his *Handbook of Musical History*, 3rd edition, edited by Alfred Einstein, I, 257 (Leipzig, Breitkopf & Härtel, 1923). As in other specimens of Greek music, "here also, except with the first word, the melodic line corresponds to the accent; here also prevails rounded, singable melody adorned with small

414

melismas. . . . The little piece is most artfully organized; it consists . . . of four sections, the two inner ones related not only by the cadenza, but also by the melodic line . . ." (H. Abert, in Adler's *Handbuch der Musikgeschichte* (1930), I, 67).

A translation would be:

> As long as you live, Phainus,
> Keep off any grief.
> Short is measured the life,
> And time, quite early, sets the limit.

3. The *antiphons* belong to the plainest forms within the Gregorian chant. They are closely allied with psalmody, and therefore are found chiefly in the secondary divine services, such as vespers. The antiphon seems originally to have been repeated as a sort of refrain after each verse of a psalm. In the Middle Ages it was always sung once at the beginning and once at the end of the psalm. It is essentially choral song. It often happens that one and the same antiphonal melody serves several texts; it is then shortened or lengthened, as the case may be. Our example is taken from the liturgy of the fourth Sunday in *Quadragesima* (Lent), and is written in the first ecclesiastical mode.

4. The *Alleluia* with its verse (V.) belongs to the most ornamented melismatic liturgical song. It is solo-singing, but with participation by the choir. In our example the soloist first sings the initial part up to the sign ⊕, then the choir repeats this part, while adding the melisma which belongs to the last syllable. The verse is rendered up to the sign ⊕ by the soloist, and from then on to the end by the choir. Thereupon the Alleluia is again repeated up to the sign by the soloist, and only its melismatic extension is sung by the choir. Thus the whole constitutes a *da capo* form, yet the rounding-off frequently — as in this case — goes even further, in that the melody of the verse flows out into

that of the Alleluia. The Alleluia has its liturgical position in the Mass between the Epistle and the Gospel.
Our example belongs to Whitsunday liturgy, and is
written in the second ecclesiastical mode.

5. The *sequence* was sung during the Mass right
after the Alleluia; and indeed it took the place of the
repetition of the Alleluia after the verse. It is to some
extent a more widely amplified form of this Alleluia,
and could, as a matter of fact, be vocalized without a
text. As to our sequence (which was published in
A. Schubiger's *The St. Gall School of Singers*, 1858)
we can say with certainty that its text was composed
by the monk of St. Gall, Notker Balbulus (d. 912), for
a pre-existing melody. It is a consecrational sequence.
The sequence consists of a series of phrases that are
repeated in pairs and are sung by the two halves of the
choir in alternation; an introductory and a concluding
part remain outside of the repetitions and are sung by
the entire choir. The sequences very often overstep
the bounds of the ecclesiastical modes, as in this case.

6. The piece is a " *conductus* " — that is, a composition the text of which has a rhythmic verse-form. The
text, according to L. Delisle, deals with the accession
to the throne of Richard the Lionhearted (1189). The
piecé is here taken from two manuscripts in Florence
and Wolfenbüttel which give chiefly works from the
Parisian " School of Notre-Dame." In a manuscript of
Roman de Fauvel from the fourteenth century, the
basic melody of our composition is found in a somewhat divergent form, with the travestied text *Floret fex
Favellea*. In this version which, contrary to ours, is
mensurably notated, there is also the syllabic part in the

" first mode " (*Floret fex Favellea* $= | \, \flat \, \sqcap \, \flat \, | \, \flat \, \sqcap \, |$)
but the manner of writing of our manuscripts, although
not mensurable, nevertheless rather points towards
the submitted rhythmification. We offer only the first

stanza; there is another to be sung to the same music, and then two more to be sung to other music (see the complete text in *Analecta Hymnica* 21, 177). The parallel thirds in the third verse and the symmetrical construction of the melisma are musically noteworthy.

7. We know that the art of the troubadours and trouvères of the twelfth and thirteenth centuries fostered various styles: in the purely lyric sphere, the lovesong (" *canso* "), the political or moralizing song (*sirventés*), the crusade-song (*ennui* and *plainte*), the disputation (*tenso* or *jeu-parti*), and in the more narrative or dramatically inclined sphere the morning song (*alba*), the *chansons d'histoire* or *de toile*, the romance, the pastourelle, and the dance-song. We give as example a love-song — the most common form — that is taken from a thirteenth-century *Chansonnier* (Paris, Bibliotèque Nationale f. franç. 20,000); it is to be found in facsimile and translation in Jean Beck's *La Musique des Troubadours* (1910). One feels clearly that this melodic blossom has sprung from popular soil, but one also senses its fine individual fragrance. If one wishes to analyse it, the arrangement of rhyme and motif couldn't be simpler; the key fluctuates between the Mixolydian mode and G major. The translated text reads:

> *When the nightingale spreads her song abroad*
> *That delights us with its melody,*
> *Then with my lovely, sweet friend*
> *I feel my heart singing in unison.*
> *Sometimes I implore her,*
> *For never yet did I love her so;*
> *Well do I know she forgets me,*
> *It is the end of my happiness.*

Two more strophes follow in the original manuscript.

8. We choose as an example of a Meistersinger tune the *Morning Song* of Hans Sachs, shoemaker-poet of

417

Nuremberg, ten of whose melodies have been handed down to us in their authentic composition in the famous Zwickauer Sachs manuscripts. Three more are to be found in the song-book of Adam Puschman at Breslau. Our *Morning Song* was made in 1518. It belongs to the Mixolydian mode (in our language, a G major without F sharp). The two verses of the opening section are followed by the end section, also divided into two, and then a third verse forms the conclusion. It is a "devotional" song, composed like a psalm and also like a melody, with minute consideration for the rhyme-structure, and yet of a free and exalted character, sparing and effective in its "*Blumen*" or embellishments. In the reading and rhythmification, which are not to be taken too seriously, I have in general followed the proposals of Hugo Riemann (*Handbook of Musical History*, II, 1. p. 480), not without comparing them to G. Münzer's version, true to the original, in *The Song-book of Adam Puschman* (Leipzig, 1906).

9. The *motet*, the popular art-form, in several parts, of the thirteenth century, consists in the combination of, as a rule, *three* different melodies: the lower part (tenor) usually taken from the store of liturgical song and rendered by some such instrument as violin or hand-organ, and two upper voices built over it, each of which sang its own text. The lower of these two voices was called the motet, from which the entire composition took its name; the upper one was the triplum. Our example shows the prevailing inclination of the times for combining the most absolutely heterogeneous elements. A naïve love-song, the confession of a sociable glutton, and a church melody, in this case a fragment from the gradual, *Propter Veritatem*, are forced together into a whole that one does well to avoid playing on the piano, lest the effect be even more frightful. For the composer, in putting the three parts together, concerned himself only with seeing that each measure be-

gan with a keynote; the tone-movement of the accompanying part follows without much regard for
consonance. The little piece comes from a Bamberg
manuscript; in another manuscript it has the same tenor
(but with a burlesqued French text: a drinking-song!),
the same middle voice, and an entirely different upper
voice; still another manuscript has it composed for four
voices (quadruplum), a fourth voice being inserted between the motet and the triplum (see P. Aubry: *Cent
Motets du XIII⁰ siècle*, 1908).

10. This *ballata* by Gio. da Cascia shows the individual vivacity which distinguished the *Ars nova* of the
fourteenth century. Judging by its text, it belongs to
the species of the so-called masquerade, of which we
offer an example further on (No. 17); but it is far removed from the frivolity typical of later times; in its
second part especially it already breathes the spirit of
the Schubertian *Organ-grinder*. The manuscript sources
of the piece are: Paris, Bibl. Nat. f. ital. 568, fol. 42;
ibid., nouv. acq. f. franç. 6771 (Codex Reina), fol.
27ᵛ–28ʳ; a third is found in Florence, Bibl. Naz., Pan-
ciatichi 26, fol. 48. The pattern of the Italian ballata
(corresponding to the French virelai) is a,b,b,a,a, with
the last part also textually similar to the first (refrain).
The translated text reads as follows:

*I am a pilgrim who wanders through the world
Asking for alms for God's mercy's sake.
I come singing with the lovely voice,
The fair countenance, and the blond curls.
Nought have I with me save my staff and purse,
And though I cry aloud, no echo answers;
And when it seems my bark sails with the wind,
Then storms cast me about in all directions.
I am a pilgrim, etc.*

11. Next to the Italian ballata we place a ballade by
the most famous representative of the *Ars nova* in

France. The sources are: Paris, Bibl. Nat. f. franç. 22-546, fol. 144ʳ; ibid., nouv. acq. franç. 6771, fol. 72ʳ; ibid., f. ital. 568, fol. 120ᵛ. The "triplum," the upper voice to this composition, is found only in the second-mentioned manuscript, but in its abrupt, jerky rhythm it is entirely homogeneous with the two lower voices. Who, upon hearing such bold, personally expressive music, can still talk of "primitive art"! The piece is in three parts, its musical garb being most delicately adapted to the poetic form: two double lines, a further double line, and a pointed concluding line; the single expression depends particularly on the surpassing of *linear* stresses through sharpened leading-note (double leading notes) and retarding effects. The translation of the first stanza reads:

> *Of all the flowers and fruits of my garden*
> *Only a single rose is left standing.*
> *All the rest were destroyed and ruined through*
> *Fortune,*
> *That cherishes bitter hostility against this fair*
> *flower,*
> *In order to let its colour and fragrance perish.*
> *But if I should see it plucked or stripped of its*
> *leaves —*
> *I would never again wish to call any other my*
> *own.*

Essential to the ballade form are the three stanzas, the division in the first part of the stanza, and the fact that the conclusion to the stanza ("*Autre après . . .*") is a refrain.

In 1926 the piece was reprinted from richer source-material by Friedrich Ludwig in the publications of the German Musical Society I (*Musikalische Werke von G. de Machaut*, p. 35); the two latter stanzas are to be found there.

Notes

12. The short section of a Mass by the Burgundian composer Gilles Binchois is to be found in the Trent Codex 92, f. 102, and was published in its original form by R. von Ficker in *Denkmäler der Tonkunst in Öster-reich*, Year 31, Vol. 61, p. 50. It is a *coloured* choral *cantus firmus* in its upper part, accompanied by two subsidiary parts, to be found in its original form in Mass XVIII of the Editio Vaticana (*Graduales*); the notes of the choral *cantus firmus* are set off by crosses. Religiosity and artistic freedom unite in this form of composition, which is much livelier than the rather stiff *cantus firmus* treatment of the sixteenth century.

13. The *frottola* of the Veronese priest Michele Pesenti represents for this collection the typical four-teenth- and fifteenth-century accompanied song, in the form of a little ballade (*ballatella*). How lucid the structure of the gay little piece is (a,b,a,b,a), how ex-actly the melody follows the rhyming chainwork of the stanza, so that each verse has its proper turn of expression! The piece is very characteristic in tone in that the lover doesn't take his own reproaches very seriously, but is playing at comedy. The accompani-ment to the vocal part was entrusted to three viols, but there was nothing to prevent its being interpreted by some keyed or plucked instrument. In such matters the times allowed complete liberty of execution.

14. The *Spring Song* of Ludwig Senfl, although printed thirty years later than the *frottola*, embodies an almost older conception of form. Pesenti sets the free and individually contrived melody in the upper voice, while Senfl invests with subsidiary parts a tune, probably not original with him, which lies in the tenor. With much more ripeness and delicacy Senfl has created the organism of the song, building it through from the inside. With Pesenti, the secondary voices flow as if in fortuitous lines; it is like a distantly sur-mised homophony that makes use of polyphony be-

cause it still knows no other means. Senfl, through the artistic means of imitation, unites the secondary parts most intimately with the song-melody — as, for instance, bass and tenor in the first verse, soprano, tenor, and bass in the third, or all four voices with the aid of melodic inversion in the fourth; or he leads the secondary voices in free opposition to the principal voice, as at the end. His song, which expresses deep German emotion so purely and tenderly, is a true polyphonic organism.

15. The Christmas motet by the "founder of the Venetian tonal school," Adrian *Willaert*, choir-conductor at St. Mark's, illuminates the change of style which was effected at the beginning of the sixteenth century. The work, in spite of its delight in melisma, is a pure *a cappella* piece; no one of the four parts is either subordinated to or set above the others; each one imitatively takes up the motif of the separate text-divisions, and all these little tranquilly or more tersely developed passages are interwoven in almost unnoticeable transition, so clearly is the whole piece constructed even as to its fine modulations (naturally within the limits of its ecclesiastical mode, the transposed Ionic). The separate motifs are simple and adapted to song, but none the less have definite character and are also capable of the supplest inflections. — The motet was printed in the second book of Willaert's motets, and is succeeded in the original by a second part.

16. Homophony does not prevail as purely in all French chansons as it does in this delightful trilling, satirical song by the conductor of the boy choir of the Sainte-Chapelle, Paris. Here the unified, harmonious chatter of the chorus of slanderers, often in other cases the lightly handled *imitation* of modest motifs, are used to gain a humorous or starkly dramatic effect. If one looks upon the refrain of the piece as a separate division, its structure may be schematized a,b,a,b,a; it

couldn't be simpler or more expressive; and it was just that in the chanson which was so pleasing to instrumental music that it chose the chanson for its model. Moreover, in the chanson the sentimental portions are just as numerous as the frivolous ones. Our example, together with its transposition to a third below, is taken from Robert Eitner's reprint.

17. The three-part *carnival song* of the highly gifted *Giovanni Domenico del Giovane da Nola* opens the second book of his *Canzoni villanesche* of 1541. It also avails itself fully of the medium of the *villanella*, among whose practices the frequent use of pure successions of fifths is the most striking. These errors in composition are no longer awkward antiquities, as in the motet, but are fully intentional. In the villanella one generally liked to parody the over-sentimental, extravagant tone of the madrigal; and one was equally fond of gaily defying the strict rules of composition, this being started through observing the naturalistic song of the peasantry, which even today is not particular as to a few parallel fifths. — The song initiates us into carnival activities, probably in the feasting-hall of some Neapolitan nobleman. Three young persons disguised as blind beggars step up to the ladies and sing their song with a falsely woebegone air. The self-presentation as well as the apostrophizing of the ladies is typical of the carnival song since Lorenzo de' Medici's time; our example, on the other hand, is one of the few which abstains from racy double meanings. During the course of the century an operatic piece developed from the dialogizing and richer musical investiture of these songs.

18. Luca Marenzio's *madrigal* is a setting for the final verse (*commiato*) of a canzone by the poetic idol of sixteenth-century composers, Petrarch ("*Quando il soave mio fido conforto*"). Laura, the poet's dead mistress, appears to him in a dream and tries to com-

fort him and turn his thoughts from earthly to celestial things; then she vanishes, full of sweet indignation at not being able to divert him from his love. Marenzio's composition is a masterly tone-painting of the sensual-supersensual vision. The beginning of the tale by the two differently shaded four-part choirs, the weeping conveyed through chromatic turns; the sighing; the B-flat chord on "*Dolcemente*," the interweaving and entanglement of motifs at the mistress's anger, the "vanishing" portrayed by divergently aspiring scales — all this shows the utmost creative force, control and flexibility in the use of harmonic and contrapuntal means, and is compressed into a psychological picture of supreme truth and delicacy.

19. Giovanni Gabrieli's Christmas Motet shows the difference between the splendid-sounding choral *Venetian* motet and Willaert's contrapuntal motet of the Netherlands, composed for the same text. A high-pitched and a low-pitched choir of four voices each build up the motif in alternation and unison. The choirs are homophonic and self-contained in formation, but the separate parts are nevertheless executed with masterly independence. The dawn of a new harmonic comprehension proclaims itself in the transposition at "*et admirabile Sacramentum*," or in the chords of fifths, sixths, and sevenths, whose present sure application one would vainly seek in earlier church works. It would be hard to find religious solemnity and religious jubilation more artistically combined than in this early work of the great Venetian.

20. In this dance-song by *Gastoldi*, choir-conductor at Mantua, a piece of purely instrumental conception — purer, in fact, than the true contemporary instrumental dance — again finds expression in song. These "balletti" are "for singing, for playing, and for dancing"; but the verses attributed to them are merely thrown in, express nothing beyond harmless *joie de*

vivre, and regularly run out into the Fa-la refrain which accents the instrumental passage. In the form which Gastoldi gave them these dance-songs exerted the greatest influence on the idealized dance-suite, much more in Germany and England even than in Italy.

In the original printing the piece is a minor third higher.

21. The Intonation for organ by the famous Andrea Gabrieli, uncle of Giovanni Gabrieli, which appeared around 1550, contains in a nutshell all the elements of the *toccata:* the disposition of the chords; the runs apportioned to both hands, out of which, as here in the fifth and sixth measures, a rather more sharply profiled motif can imperceptibly arise. The mighty, many-membered toccata of the North- and Middle-German organ-composers evolved later on from just such origins; but it always maintained, as it does here, the appearance of improvisation.

22. If one compares the *ricercar* (or fugue with several themes) by the famous organist of St. Mark's, Venice, with Willaert's motet, the similarity of form instantly hits one in the eye, excepting that Merulo must do justice to the instrumental style by inventing somewhat more plastic themes. The weakness of this early fugal form is that the six themes are still not plastic enough and are too closely related without there being any real connexion between the various motifs. The piece is given exactly in accordance with the old printing, which doesn't bother to distinguish between the separate parts, but which, to make up for that, precisely defines the distribution of the parts between the two hands. Pauses are added in only a few places. The ornamentation is still pretty mechanical and lifeless in character; it took the seventeenth century to develop the fugal theme in which the embellishment is resolved, as it were, into the theme and belongs to the essential fabrication of the piece.

23. John Dowland's song or " ayre " " My thoughts
are winged " is a charming and characteristic example
of the transition from choral song to monody. It is
taken from the *First Booke of Songes or Ayres of
fowre partes with Tableture for the Lute: So made
that all the partes together, or either of them seuerally
may be song to the Lute, Orpherian or Viol de
gambo* . . . (London, 1597); in other words, a work
that permitted of both the " old " and the " new "
manner of execution. But it is clear that Dowland in
his heart was already on the side of monody. He was
a famous lutenist, who as such had reaped glory in
Germany, Italy, and France and had later also visited
the northern and eastern countries of Europe. But in
spite of this internationalism, his songs for the lute are
very English — indeed, such songs, whose flowering
season was very brief, not more than fifteen years, existed only in Shakespeare's England and in none of the
other musical countries of the time. This song is no
arranged canzonetta, but in its melodics and declamation is already an individual lyrical setting for a very
celebrated poem (attributed to George, Earl of Cum-
berland): the first song " To the Moon." The poem
has two more stanzas:

And you, my thoughts, that some mistrust do
    carry,
  If for mistrust my mistress do you blame,
Say, though you alter, yet you do not vary,
  As she doth change and yet remain the same.
Distrust doth enter hearts but not infect,
And love is sweetest seasoned with suspect.

If she for this with clouds do mask her eyes,
  And make the heavens dark with her disdain,
With windy sighs disperse them in the skies,

Or with thy tears dissolve them into rain,
Thoughts, hopes, and love return to me no more
Till Cynthia shine as she hath done before.

Our reprint is taken from E. H. Fellowes's excellent work: *The English School of Lutenist Song Writers*, Part I (London: Winthrop Rogers, Ltd.; 1920).

24. As example of the early primitive monodic style in opera we offer Apollo's Lament over the loss of his love, from *Dafne* by *Marco da Gagliano*, performed in Mantua in 1608. The Florentine master did not concern himself with anything beyond effective declamation; the bass is merely a support for the song and is not allowed the slightest imitative turn. But one will notice that even in this simple and almost awkward piece the structure of the recitative, conforming to the sense, already tends to round itself out into a closed composition. This cantabile, sentimental recitative actually contains the elements of the secco recitative, the arioso, and especially of the aria.

25. The *instrumental canzon* (canzon francese) of the Italianized Frenchman, Giovanni di Macque (maestro di cappella in Naples), shows with all possible conciseness the essentials of this form, from whose soil the *sonata* sprang: the fresh and unceremonious invention of motifs, their entirely unassuming execution, and the clear articulation of the whole. The elaboration of a double motif is followed by that of a quite short intermediary member (from the tenth to the fourteenth measure); then another double motif is again briefly viewed in jesting play with inversion; at the end comes a coda, in which the prolongation of the motif in the bass is also just a good joke. In the original copy, which is not preserved, surely the first section is repeated, and perhaps also the coda. The vivacious piece is taken from the tablature-book of the Heilbronner organist Johann Woltz (1617).

26. The four-part variations suite by *Paul Peuerl* (organist of the Evangelical church in Steyr, Upper Austria) comes from his *New Padouans, Intradas, Dances and Galliards* (1611), which has been reprinted (1929) in an excellent edition of the *Denkmäler der Tonkunst in Österreich* (Geiringer). They are, as it says on the title-page, " to be quite gaily used for all instrumental music " — no longer actually folk-song, but already finer chamber art for the music-lovers united in the Collegia Musica of the times. Still they are directly descended from the dance-music of the sixteenth and seventeenth centuries, which loved to create contrasted yet coherently joined pairs of dance-movements — that is, to follow up a piece in binary measure with a livelier one in triple time (*Tripla, Proportz*) made of exactly the same melodic stuff. This usage of the social dance was seized upon and refined for chamber music by a line of early seventeenth-century composers, chiefly German, who also expanded the dance-pairs into a cyclic dance-suite with unified thematic structure. The principle of character-variation is, to be sure, not their exclusive property; it permeates all European instrumental music of the century, and is equally effective in England, Italy, and France, in the canzon and in the sonata.

Our example, consisting of padouan, intrada, dance, and galliard, shows in two rhythmically contrasted pairs (binary — triple time) the progression from moderate to more and more vigorous vivacity and release, the motif material becoming ever briefer and more concentrated, without losing its discernibility. Only the padouan has three parts, the second and third of which are contracted in the following dances to a single, almost summarizing part.

27. Heinrich Schütz's *motet*, taken from the second part of the *Symphoniæ sacræ*, Op. 10, printed in Dresden, 1647, shows the concept of *concerted* music

which was realized at the beginning of the seventeenth century. Though it retains much that is outmoded in its harmonic form (not yet our G major, but still the Mixolydian mode, always tending towards the subdominant) and in its handling of instruments (to which one could just as easily affix the text, thus obtaining a rather strangely divided, one-sided motet for three voices), what is new nevertheless stares us in the face. In the first part we have the calm, steady, regular wandering of the bass, which is also such a fine poetic symbol of the worshipper's trust in God (the text is freely composed from Exodus and the Psalms). This instrumental bass, thematically fully independent, merely gives the harmonic basis for the free, arioso declamation of the voice, and the alternation of the voice with the instruments. The second part, built upon a short motif and enlivened by the concerting principle, is a rhythmically and melodically unified whole, such as the sixteenth century could not have produced.

28. The chamber cantata by Domenico Gabrielli, who worked in Modena and Bologna and was famed as a 'cellist, is a typical example of this form. Three recitative divisions, of which the last flows out into an arioso, frame two arias of *da capo* form; in the second the middle portion is more strongly contrasted than in the first. The size is still small, the coloratura still sober and expressive, which is not always the case with the contemporary and later operatic arias, whose framework is extended by the preludes and interludes of the orchestral accompaniment, and which invite the voice to contend, as it were, with some concerting instrument.

29. *John Ravencroft's* trio sonata for two violins and basso continuo (to be performed by violoncello and harpsichord) is a fine example of the old Italian church sonata in the definitive form which it received chiefly from Arcangelo Corelli. There are two pairs

of movements, each again contrastingly formed: the first " grave " is more of an introduction, with the first forte part especially giving the effect of a gate that opens solemnly and affords a view into a quiet and strictly ordered . world. The succeeding fugato expresses a more lively, but still sober and sustained feeling; the execution of the second motif is participated in too by the bass, which stated the theme only once during the first movement. The slow second movement is one of the spiritual anthems in which the best Italian composers of the period expressed their deepest, most intimate emotions; the two-part concluding allegro, with its bold moving bass and its solidity, knits itself back most skilfully into the first largo, and also affords a modest opportunity to virtuosity. — The piece was formerly attributed to the Venetian master Antonio Caldara. Erich Schenk (*Zeitschrift für Musikwissenschaft*, XII, 247) has shown that it is printed in the *Sonata a tre* (op. 1; Rome, 1695) of the English musician *John Ravenscroft;* I have revised it according to the original printing. The sonata, still under Caldara's name, underwent an excellent adaptation for practical use by Hugo Riemann (*Collegium musicum*, No. 44).

30. The French overture by *Agostino Steffani* belongs to the opera seria *Orlando Generoso*, performed in Hanover in 1691, recently reprinted in the *Denkmäler der Tonkunst in Bayern*, XII, 2 (H. Riemann). Agostino Steffani, one of the greatest style-disseminators of his time, had gone on a virtuoso's trip to Paris in the winter of 1678–9 and had become acquainted with the operatic style of his countryman G. B. Lully at its source; he had occasion to reproduce this style in very pure form at the Hanoverian court, which was particularly inclined towards French art. Yet his overture is French style with Italian colouring. Lully's overture favours five-part (not four-part) writing and

is much more unconcerned and careless in its composition than the strictly schooled Italian could readily approve. For all that, Steffani seizes upon the type exactly: the slow, weighty, solemnly pathetic introduction, with its punctuated rhythms and notes tied beyond the measure; the quick, contrasting movement beginning with a light fugato, into which the pastoral trio episode for two oboes and bassoon dovetails, after the pattern of the chaconne (Lully's final movement). When performed, the bass was to be doubled in octave.

31. The example of the "Italian" overture form is taken from Nicola Piccinni's most famous and successful opera buffa, played all over Europe, *La Buona Figliuola* (or *La Cecchina*), text by Carlo Goldoni, first performed in Rome in 1760. Such overtures were also, or mostly, called "sinfonie" (symphonies), and one will notice that they actually represent in miniature form the true chamber and concert symphonies of the time: the allegro spiritoso with a first and (after attaining to the dominant) second theme; the slower lyrical middle movement in a contrasting key; the bright, concluding presto; from such pieces, through broadening of the form and deepening of the expression, the independent symphony really developed. As our example is concerned only with the aspect of the form and not with a complete pianoforte arrangement, I have retained, according to an English copy of the work, the insufficient yet dainty clavier arrangement with which the times were satisfied. Piccinni's orchestra here consists of strings, two oboes, and two trumpets.

32. The solo sonata of the Piedmontese, G. B. Somis, who as Corelli's pupil, and Giardini's, Pugnani's, and Leclair's teacher, played an important mediating role in music, mingles elements of the church sonata with those of the chamber sonata. The slow introduction is derived from the realm of the *sonata da chiesa*, but nevertheless already breathes the spirit of intimacy.

431

The two other movements, on the other hand, are idealized two-part dance pieces, the first a kind of allemande, the second a popular rigaudon; and both have an abbreviated reprise, a recapitulation of the first part. The development is still supplied by a mere transposition of the theme into the parallel key: the dramatic duality of the sonata form was not yet clearly recognized at this date (about 1725). The sonata is reproduced from a manuscript of the Royal Domestic Library, Berlin.

33. The prelude from the third of Bach's English suites, of which the introductions to four are especially filled with the concerto spirit, represents the type of the concerto grosso more clearly and simply than perhaps any of the actual Brandenburg concertos. To the tutti is opposed a three-part concertino, entrusted perhaps to flute, viola, and violoncello. One can easily see from the composition how much the later sonata form owes to the concerto: the prepared recapitulation is already foreshadowed, the dramatic interchange between tutti and solo paves the way for the development, and the foretaste becomes particularly marked when, as in our example, the concertino motif contrasts with the stormy, energetic main theme of the tutti. — Be it expressly noted that the performance of the piece on Bach's double harpsichord also admits of another dynamic interpretation.

34. In the little clavier-suite by J. K. F. Fischer, kapellmeister of the margrave of Baden, the contents of the suite, as fixed by Froberger in the order of allemande, courante, sarabande, gigue, are abandoned for a gayer and freer selection of dances after the modern French pattern. A placid prelude, gliding through two motifs — which can typify for this collection the free forms of clavier literature — is followed by a passacaglia in rondo form (of course far removed from the concept of a variations suite over a basso ostinato which

Bach associated with the name passacaglia); then a gay bourrée and a fashionable minuet. The most important part of this minor art is the ornamentation: the trill without grace-note (ᴧᴠ), the semi-trill or mordent (ᴧᴠ) that touches the lower neighbouring note once, and the combination of these two embellishments (ᴧᴧᴠ). The *Musikalische Blumenbüschlein*, from which our example comes, is to be found together with Fischer's other works for clavier and organ in a careful reprint by E. von Werra.

35. The little *choral arrangement* of Johann Pachelbel shows in a nutshell the form of the introductory movement which Johann Sebastian Bach chose for the greater number of his choral cantatas, only with him the orchestra adds its profound word to the relationship between the three lower voices and the chorale. The melody of our chorale comes from Nicolaus Selneccer's *Christian Psalms* (1587); the first verse of the accompanying poem by Ludwig Helmboldt reads:

> *Now God the Lord allows us*
> *To thank Him and revere Him*
> *For all His gifts*
> *That we have received;*

and it was certainly before Pachelbel's eyes when he composed his prelude. Pachelbel ushers in the first line with a fugato that uses the abridged introductory motif of the chorale; for the rest, the lower parts express in intimate and lively turns the exultation of a grateful heart; the mordent is in this sense very characteristic. At the end Pachelbel has again remembered the last lines of the poem:

> *Preserve us in the truth,*
> *Give us eternal freedom*
> *To praise thy name,*
> *Through Jesus Christ, Amen.*

36. The buffo aria of G. B. Pergolesi belongs to the intermezzo *La Serva Padrona* (*The Maid Turned Mistress*), which the then twenty-three-year-old Neapolitan master had himself composed for his opera seria *Il Prigonier Superbo*, performed August 28, 1733, and which was destined to play a yet unsuspected role in operatic history; it has remained alive up to our time. The intermezzi, which later took the name of *opere buffe*, were neither dramatically nor musically related to the opere serie, between whose three acts they were inserted (thence the traditional two acts of the Italian opera buffa); they were to be nothing more than a lively interlude. The *Serva Padrona* is played by only two singing characters, to which is added the role of the dumb servant: the tyrannical but graceful maid Serpina by means of a trick wrests a promise of marriage from her rich bachelor employer, Uberto: a puppet's comedy with the most delicate realistic features. Our aria is Serpina's first: charming in the grace with which the girl bewitches the old man, each melodic turn born of a dramatic gesture, each motif brief, variable, piquant — the monumental aria-form filled with quite new life and spirit. The whole work has been available since 1925 in one of K. Geiringer's careful and excellent pocket-edition scores.

37. The fragment from the first finale (Act II) of Mozart's *Le Nozze di Figaro* (*The Marriage of Figaro*) gives an idea of how opera buffa succeeded in representing a complicated dramatic action " with intensified life, so to speak, highest truth to nature, and the greatest ideal distinctness, all at once " — and, we may add, without in any way sacrificing the solidity and beauty of the absolute musical form.

All the hypotheses of the situation need not be given here. Suffice it to say that Count Almaviva, who lays traps for Susanna, his wife's maid, stakes everything on deferring Susanna's marriage to his valet Figaro. But

Figaro, who has set a counter-trap, parries all the
Count's thrusts; and the Count, who in the scene before
our finale, alone confronts the confederate women and
Figaro, feels himself completely driven into a corner:
" *tutto, tutto è un mistero per me* " — " all this is a mystery to me." There is a general pause for his discom-
fiture and the triumph of the two women and Figaro.

Here our scene begins: Marcellina, who has an un-
redeemed promissory note of Figaro's, and a promise
of marriage in case of debt, enters with her ally Basilio
(the Count's house-priest) and Dr. Bartolo, her lawyer.

There are seven people on the stage: the Count as
arbitrator in the middle, right and left the two hostile
trios. Then the ordered turbulence of the opening
scene: Marcellina's party loudly and resolutely claims
a hearing. And now there follows in the answering
quartet the finest characterization of situation and of
individual personages. The Count drawing a breath of
relief, almost silently rejoicing; Figaro deliberating but
also outdone, by no means out of countenance, yet
somewhat depressed; the two women, each separately
(and not together) more excited; Susanna sets in later,
going from the dominant into the tonic, while the
Countess, starts in the tonic and lands in the dominant.
Susanna sees a way out that is still unknown to the
troubled Countess. (One must not think that something is here " stuck in " — the greatest depth and consistency prevail in such a masterpiece.) Now the scene
begins to fall into order: Figaro's protests; the Count's
soothing attempts; statements by Marcellina, Bartolo,
Basilio, all hotly contested, all three advancing from a
serious to a chattering tone; finally a complete reversal
in the situation: the Count rules, Figaro's side is excited,
Marcellina's side is fully conscious of victory. The
scene ends in the real " *stretta* " of the finale (printed
only in the first few measures), which leaves the parties
confronting each other in the greatest agitation —

435

without a solution, for of course a third and fourth act are to follow.

38. Haydn's quartet movement is the first movement of the second of those " Russian " or "*Jungfer* " quartets, with which Haydn in 1781, after a ten year's pause in his production of quartets, established the " special new method " of work as principle of the sonata form. A characteristic of this principle is the economy of the melodic material. No one of the four instruments says anything indifferent, anything unrelated to the unified, collective character of the movement. The main motif in the theme of our movement is the little fanfare motif with which the first violin begins: the expression of a happy and hearty will-to-life, in whose melodic program the other three instruments then thoroughly concur, to take it up later themselves. With a common, intersupporting impetus, the movement leads into the second theme (twenty-first measure), in which a firm goal seems to have been happily reached, and which after two reflective passages is jubilantly stated. In the ending of the last four measures the first motif sets forth its deep satisfaction with what has been accomplished. — But the real examination is first to be found in the development, which here consists of almost as many measures as the first part. The 'cello, then the first violin, wish to take up the work, but the rhythmic motif that at first was concurring and supporting now brings about restraint. This must be overcome by a vigorous attack in the solid subdominant; everything works powerfully together, and within six measures the recapitulation in the basic key is already apparently attained (this " false recapitulation," " *fausse reprise*," is one of the legacies which Haydn inherited from Philipp Emanuel Bach, yet which, as in this case, he endlessly enriched). But only apparently. The first violin itself immediately becomes timid, the second violin and the viola add their uncertainty, and now

begins the real fight, which reveals the *character* of the contestants, and which finally culminates in the four menacing broken beats. The main theme in C flat displays the full gravity of the strife, but also brings the solution, the " Steady! " and only now can the recapitulation set in with its full musical and spiritual effect. And there is no end to the pleasure and admiration one has in tracing the little modifications in spirit and character that Haydn's resources have brought about in it.

39. The *recitativo accompagnato* (accompanied recitative) from Act II, Scene 3, of Gluck's *Iphigenie en Tauride* (Paris, May 18, 1779) is chosen as the final example for this collection because it contains in embryo form the entire development of the opera, and not only of the opera, but also of the song, the ballade, and the symphonic composition of the nineteenth century. Fundamentally it seems to be only an intensification of secco recitative into the grandiose and the pathetic, but it is something more. It shows the new function of the *orchestra*, which portrays not only the external situation, but also the inner movements of the characters who stand on the stage. Orestes, his mother's murderer, is alone in the prison of the Scythian barbarians, and sees the death for which he longs staring him in the face. The introductory *grave* paints in six measures the entire tumult of his soul: mounting resolution, rising terror, artificial courage; in the recitative a wild agitation, then sudden benumbed quiet — an *apparent* quiet. For in the following aria the pounding and boring of the orchestra contradicts the sense of the text: Orestes would like to persuade himself that he is absolved, but the orchestra shows us that the Eumenides, the avenging goddesses, are not yet through — and they appear to him indeed in grimmest form in the following scene. The orchestra tells us what the hero on the stage doesn't know; the orchestra, the accompaniment,

is his conscience. Without the enhanced role of the "accompaniment" the development of the romantic opera and of all other song forms of the nineteenth century would be unthinkable. Even formally the *accompagnato* conquers all these styles: it has a dissolving disintegrating tendency which the aria, the song-principle, must always resist; until in Wagner's "*Gesamt-kunstwerk*" the symphonic principle, the orchestra, has become the main thing, to which the voice is often subordinated or at best related on equal terms.

INDEX

i